# Recognizing Rural Ministry

# Recognizing Rural Ministry

*Moving from Anecdotal Assumptions to Data Derived Opportunities*

CARL P. GREENE

*Foreword by Jeffrey Clark*

WIPF & STOCK · Eugene, Oregon

RECOGNIZING RURAL MINISTRY
Moving from Anecdotal Assumptions to Data Derived Opportunities

Wipf & Stock
An Imprint of Wipf and Stock Publishers
199 W. 8th Ave., Suite 3
Eugene, OR 97401

www.wipfandstock.com

PAPERBACK ISBN: 978-1-6667-4923-6
HARDCOVER ISBN: 978-1-6667-4924-3
EBOOK ISBN: 978-1-6667-4925-0

SEPTEMBER 8, 2022 3:15 PM

In memory of my grandfather, Arlie L. Greene (1919–2017), who taught me how to tell a good story, and more importantly, how to listen to a story to make it good. He died in the same farmhouse that he was born in—a life goal that portrays his deep rural roots. In this constancy of place, he also taught me that transformative change can happen late in life.

# Contents

# SECTION 3

# List of Figures and Tables

## FIGURES

## TABLES

# Foreword

IN the field of rural ministry, a growing number of books have been published in recent years. Many of these books have been written with the idea of "here is what I did to see breakout growth in my rural setting, and here is how you can do the same." While these books may provide examples and ideas for rural ministry, we need more books concerning rural work written from more theological and more academic perspectives.

Carl Greene's book provides deep insight into an overlooked issue, not only in rural churches but in the greater church world here in North America- reaching the segment of people he calls "early old age." Greene includes people from roughly 65 years old to 80 years old to be early old age.

Carl's book was especially poignant for me since I am quickly approaching this demographic segment. I see my peers just as he described, in relatively good health, seeking ways to give back to their communities, and possessing a greater spiritual interest than ever before. Yet when churches begin to talk about senior adult ministry the conversation invariably drifts toward ministry for those over 80 with an emphasis on shut-ins and widows.

Carl offers intriguing ministry insights for those between middle age and the typical description of old age. He goes into detail describing the early old age demographic segment and offers suggestions how to address this often-overlooked section by rural churches.

This book is a must read for those seeking to address their rural community from a missional perspective. It addresses a gap in ministry strategy often overlooked and presents a tremendous opportunity available to rural churches to reach early old agers for Christ.

# Preface

F OR most of my life, I have been confident that I know what rural is, and therefore have a firm grasp of how rural ministry works. I have rarely made such a bombastic statement explicitly, but internally, I have been silently confident of my expertise. Afterall, I have lived in rural towns since 1974, I should know a thing or two.

Then something changed. I do not think that it was simply part of a midlife crisis of identity. There was something else going on. I increasingly discovered how much I do not know about rural ministry. Rather than continuing to assume that my rural ministry experience was ubiquitous throughout America, I began searching for tools to study rural ministry contexts.

This was not a cognitive, step-by-step process, but a lived story of discovery. I grew up on my family's dairy farm in a wonderful rural town in upstate New York. I returned to that same town of 1900 people after college to be an active lay leader in my home church. I became a partner in my family's dairy farm, served as an elected official in small town government, was active in civic organizations, and joined an organization to lobby for farm and rural interests in Albany, NY and Washington, DC. I grew in confidence of knowing what mattered to rural America.

After 15 years on the farm and increasingly delving into local vocational ministry opportunities, my family and I responded to a call to pastor in North-Central Pennsylvania. We moved to a town of 600 people in a county of just over 17,000 people. There was a clear farm presence in the town, and there were even some farmers in the church. A perfect fit that we had been prepared for—or so I thought.

I served the small country church while I completed seminary. After completing seminary, I continued serving the church that initially called us, and went on to simultaneously serve as a Hospice Chaplain for a hospital system covering four rural counties. I also served as an interim pastor or pulpit supply for a number of churches representing a wide variety of denominations. The broader my interaction, the more my rural expertise seemed to erode.

I began to realize that my many assumptions about rural experience were far from reality. My hometown in Upstate New York was not nearly the same experience as in Pennsylvania (traveling nearly one hour to get to the closest Walmart was a new remoteness experience).

Light bulb moment—I am not a rural expert. I read a number of rural ministry books, but often times came away frustrated that my little church was not blossoming into the thriving, enviable church of rapid growth and name recognition that the books described could happen in my town. I longed to learn tools to study my rural context rather than force someone else's innovation into my own ministry calling.

I began to realize that I need to listen to the experts of my community (the residents) to learn. The hunger for learning grew, and I returned to school one more time, this time to pursue my PhD at Trinity International University just outside Chicago, IL. My family and I were intimidated by the greater Chicago vibe, so we settled in the middle of corn fields in southern Wisconsin. This time, a town of 800 people, but in a county of over 160,000. Once again, the rural experience was far different than the previous two stops on our family's sojourn.

These disparate experiences influenced my dissertation research. Rather than approaching rural ministry as a monolithic experience, I wanted to develop assessment tools that respect the diversity of rural experiences. I also wanted to delve into some overlooked ministry opportunities that demographic data points to, but the rural church has been slow to respond to. The book that you are now reading contains some of the fruit of my research—hopefully a readable text that still maintains an academic foundation that is deeply rooted in data.

Much of the data utilized by this book builds from my dissertation research: fifty qualitative interviews, including thirty-one rural resident interviews and nineteen pastor or ministry leader interviews. There were twenty-eight different churches represented in the interviews, connected with nine different denominations, conferences, or independent church status. My dissertation research was also informed by a previous qualitative study that I had conducted involving a single network of churches where I conducted 2 focus groups, 11 site observations, and 23 personal interviews.

The unique contribution of book is the development of research tools that reveal the complexity of the rural context while simultaneously examining specificities of how aging shapes believing, belonging, and behaving in a variety of rural settings. The academic foundation of this book is intended to offer college students, seminarians, and ministry certificate students a unique resource to utilize specifically for rural ministry training. The rural ministry tools suggested in this book are intentionally developed for rural pastors and lay leaders searching for ways to listen for the needs and opportunities presented by the people of their community.

There are outstanding rural ministry books available. Hopefully my book provides an academic contribution to the conversations generated by other authors who have rich experiences and insights. Even more, I dream that my book sparks further academic research of the rural ministry context and facilitates the development of better tools to help us study the complex opportunities that abound in rural ministry. May God be glorified as we join Him in his missional Kingdom work throughout rural America.

# Acknowledgements

I HESITATE to write acknowledgements, because it is impossible to include everyone whom should be here. Given that disclaimer, I tip my hat to three primary groups. First, my family: Cindy, Seth, Luke, Samuel, and Elizabeth. You have endured car rides that included monologues about rural ministry and gerontology. You picked up and moved halfway across the country as a part of a PhD journey. You have loved me deeply throughout the process. Even while you have sacrificed throughout this family journey, you have been my primary long-suffering champions. I would be remiss if I did not tip my hat to our eldest son Seth who had the misfortune of agreeing to serve as my book manuscript reader and advisor. Thank you for running the marathon with me.

The second group that I would like to specifically thank are my dissertation reviewers at Trinity International University, Deerfield, IL. My dissertation director, Dr. David Gustafson, my second reader, Dr. Manuel Rauchholz, and the ICS Program Director, Dr. Craig Ott; all went above and beyond to move my research into dissertation form. All three invested in me, not just my work, through coursework prior to the dissertation, and have subsequently provided guiding insights, encouragement, and critique that I continue to benefit from. I specifically thank Dr. Gustafson for providing me with the privilege to serve as his Graduate Assistant. That experience galvanized my research trajectory and opened new doors of opportunity that provided life skills I would not have otherwise possessed. You even went on to encourage me to adapt the dissertation into a published book. Third, thank you to the rural residents and pastors who participated in the research. Not only are you gracious and fascinating conversation partners, but your passion to point others to your dynamic, growing faith is contagious.

# List of Abbreviations

| APC | Age, Period, and Cohort |
|---|---|
| Metro | Metropolitan |
| Nonmetro | Nonmetropolitan |
| RUCC | Rural-Urban Continuum Codes |
| SBNR | Spiritual but Not Religious |
| SOC | Selective Optimization with Compensation |
| SST | Socioemotional Selectivity Theory |
| USDA ERS | United States Department of Agriculture Economic Research Service |

# CHAPTER 1

# The Mann Gulch Wildfire of 1949

## THE STORY

AUGUST 5, 1949. A wildfire started in Mann Gulch of Montana's Helena National Forest that burned nearly five thousand acres of woods and grasslands.[1] When the fire was first spotted by plane, it was estimated to be an ordinary "ground fire" that was slowly advancing.[2] The crew of fifteen sent in to fight this fire were confident that they could have it contained quickly and efficiently.[3] And this was not just any crew being sent in, it was a crew of elite firefighters: the Smokejumpers.[4]

The U.S. Forest Service started sending Smokejumpers to fight inaccessible forest fires in 1940. Smokejumpers parachute in with their tools and begin fighting a fire before it expands beyond a controllable size and intensity. The Smokejumpers had developed a reputation across their nine years as elite firefighters in the Forest Service ranks.[5] Not only were they effective, but they seemed invincible. Despite falling from the sky and landing on rocks and in trees in the face of danger, not a single Smokejumper had perished fighting a wildfire prior to 1949.[6]

On August 5th, 1949, 15 Smokejumpers leapt from their C-47 to fight the fire in Mann Gulch. The Smokejumpers had a relatively uneventful

---

1. Lehman, "August 5, 1949: Mann Gulch Tragedy."
2. Maclean, *Young Men and Fire*, 33.
3. Maclean, *Young Men and Fire*, 61.
4. Grant, *Think Again*, 1.
5. Maclean, *Young Men and Fire*, 19.
6. Maclean, *Young Men and Fire*, 57, 269. Lehman, "August 5, 1949."

landing about one-half-mile from the fire. The crew collected their air-dropped supplies and met up with a fire guard from a nearby campground who was fighting the fire singlehandedly.[7] When the crew moved from their cargo area around 5:00 pm they were still not alarmed by the fire—it was limited in size and intensity.[8]

Before the Smokejumpers were able to start fighting the fire, the crew's foreman, Wagner Dodge, noted that the fire had jumped its previous boundaries, so the plans to contain the fire were shelved and developing an escape route became the primary concern. By 5:45 pm the fire was roaring up to thirty feet high, and Dodge turned the crew around to begin the race up a steep slope to reach the safety over a ridge. As Mann Gulch became engulfed in flames, two of the Smokejumpers were fast enough to make the dash of seven hundred yards to safety.[9] One Smokejumper found a place of safety. In just a matter of minutes, the race to escape was over. By 5:57 pm, thirteen perished and only three survived.[10]

## A SHARED TRAGEDY

This story is a catastrophe. As author Norman Maclean advocates, we cannot erase the catastrophic aspects, but we can move the story to a "remembered tragedy" where we discern life applications for today.[11] There is something in this for us as rural pastors, ministry leaders, and congregants as we move from surviving the catastrophic events of the last few years to a "remembered tragedy" where we thrive in ministry because we are moving to a healthier place.[12] From COVID to social upheaval to financial challenges, the list is long in regard to harrowing events we have faced. Learning from our shared tragedy is required for health as we face future fires together.

There are three lessons from this remembered wildfire tragedy that I want us to consider as rural residents leading through this season of crisis:

7. Lehman, "August 5, 1949."

8. Maclean, *Young Men and Fire*, 57.

9. Grant, *Think Again*, 1–2. Maclean, *Young Men and Fire*, 269. Two of the smoke-jumpers survived a brief time before succumbing to the effects of their burns.

10. Lehman, "August 5, 1949."

11. Maclean, *Young Men and Fire*, 46.

12. Numerous applications of this can be observed in recent literature: Grant, *Think Again*; Weick, "Drop Your Tools," 301–13.

1) Drop your tools; 2) Practice Communication; 3) Fight the right fight. The chapters in Section 1 of the book deal with dropping tools given that our default is to hold on to the wrong identity in rural ministry. The chapters about communication in Section 2 define rural ministry terms that we assume we all agree on (but don't). Section 3 chapters about fighting the right fight push us to examine how we as ministry practitioners generate rural ministry barriers on a daily basis.

# SECTION 1

# CHAPTER 2

# Drop Your Tools

B Y the time the Smokejumpers landed in Mann Gulch, the fire had grown to sixty acres from its spotted size of six acres, but was still confined to the ridge.[1] Due to conditions surrounding the drop, the cargo was scattered around the hillside and extra time was required to collect tools and supplies.[2] Tragically, at this point in the story the Smokejumpers saw their primary job as fire control and responsibility to the crew and safety as a distant second.[3]

Since the focus was on fire control, a series of small, but tragic decisions took place when minutes made a world of difference. First, the crew started running later than they should have under these conditions.[4] Second, there was a delay in an order to drop the heavy tools and equipment being carried.[5] Third, and perhaps most tragic, some Smokejumpers did not drop their tools even after the command was made by the foreman.[6]

Let's pause here for a moment. At 5:45 pm the crew had turned around and started to run. It was not until 5:53 pm that the command to drop tools took place. Some had already tossed their heavy packs, but some refused even after the command. But why hold their tools when things were already getting desperate?

1. Turner, "Thirteenth Fire," 27.
2. Maclean, *Young Men and Fire*, 57.
3. Maclean, *Young Men and Fire*, 217.
4. Maclean, *Young Men and Fire*, 5.
5. Maclean, *Young Men and Fire*, 71.
6. Maclean, *Young Men and Fire*, 73.

We hold our tools because it is our default response. In fact, it is not just a physical response, but holding our tools is also an allegory of our response whenever we find ourselves in danger.[7] A lack of holistic identity drives us to hold our tools.[8]

*Identity.* When you drop your tools, you are admitting failure—and you do not want to do that too soon.[9] This failure gets wrapped up into identity. The tools of the firefighter are part of who they are and what they do—laying them down is not simply setting down an implement, it is setting aside who they are and what they are called to do.[10] Research has demonstrated in a number of settings that tools become part of our identity, and many of us will continue to run with extra weight. As in Mann Gulch, people carry their tools even though every second matters.[11] In Mann Gulch, they were within sight of a safe area, but did not reach it due to the extra weight.[12] They were firefighters with iconic tools for the work. They were slow to gain the necessary nimbleness by recognizing purpose and identity change.[13]

This brings us to an opportunity to reflect on our ministry roles and ask some key questions. As rural pastors, ministry leaders, and congregants, what tools do we hold on to due to identity? After experiencing the last few years, what are the "tools" that you are no longer carrying? Which ones should stay dropped and which ones get picked up again?

These questions are critical for us to consider. There are ministry tools that we have been carrying that no longer fit our current context—certain modes of communication, expectations of the church always functioning in its gathered state rather than scattered, and the list goes on. At the same time, there have been certain tools that we have dropped, such as certain inter-personal interaction, that need to be picked up once again. Intentionality matters when it comes to our tools—where we wear God's missional call in the present over the church identity we would like to project.

7. Weick, "Drop Your Tools," 301.

8. Weick, "Drop Your Tools," 308.

9. Weick, "Drop Your Tools," 307.

10. Weick, "Drop Your Tools," 308.

11. Maclean, *Young Men and Fire*, 226.

12. Weick, "Drop Your Tools," 301.

13. Grant, *Think Again*, 7.

# CHAPTER 3

# Holding on to the Wrong Identity

W HEN we talk about church outreach, what groups do we instantly gravitate towards? Youth and young families certainly get all sorts of attention, and for good reason. That span of life is a spiritually sensitive window for people to come to a saving knowledge of Jesus Christ. The age four to fourteen window is referred to repeatedly in most conversations about our outreach focus. Another group that gets a lot of attention are spiritual none's—the younger generations of America that are being raised without any connection to church or knowledge of Jesus Christ. Once again, this is a fantastic group to reach—people in desperate need of Jesus.

A question though—are there groups of people churches are overlooking in rural America? Groups that are assumed to receive plenty of attention, but end up being missed by intentional outreach? This is where we come to the question of people entering early old age—the window of time where adults retire yet have more years of active, healthy life ahead.

More specifically, early old age refers to the "young-old" age category that baby boomers have entered into or are on the verge of entering into as of the writing of this book. Early old age refers to a generally recognized postretirement time period stretching from age 65 to 80. This is the time of life in which there is increased freedom, yet precedes a number of "care-dependency needs" that rise more dramatically after age 80.[1] In many ways, given changes in mortality and the health and functionality of this age-bracket compared to 100 years ago, there is a new "robust elderly" age

1. Dillon and Wink, *In the Course of a Lifetime*, 137.

class.[2] Yet, the specific study of religion within this young-old time period has been minimal and has generated little documentation.[3]

The baby boomer generation (born 1946–1964) does not capture church ministry headlines in the 21st century.[4] In contrast, there has been tremendous interest devoted to the previously mentioned trends of young adults who are leaving Christian churches, are disaffiliating from Christian religion, or practicing religion differently than previous generations.[5] This focus on the young reflects that there has been an overall increase in emphasis on the opportunity to engage with the unchurched who are more willing to hear about Christian beliefs than previously assumed.[6] What if the unchurched are not only the young?

Baby boomers left the church in unprecedented numbers[7] and are now showing interest in returning. Yet, most of the time, when we refer to ministry to mature adults, it is ministry to shut-ins and those with unmet needs. There is little intentional effort made to reach baby-boomers as they transition to older age lifestyles. "As it is, older people's spiritual needs tend to be rather neglected, not least by religious ministers, who can appear sometimes over-focused on evangelisation to younger people."[8]

In fact, a preponderance of older adults attending a small membership church is generally considered to be due to a *lack* of evangelism—that all that is left in the church are those who grew up there and never left. While that is sadly often the case, it is not the only explanation. Could a sea of silver hair in a congregation be an indication of effective evangelism and

---

2. Carey, "Life Span: A Conceptual Overview," 12.

3. Dillon and Wink, *In the Course of a Lifetime*, 137.

4. The concept of each generation having a general pattern and characteristics gained a great deal of salience in popular culture with North American books such as: Strauss and Howe, *Generations: The History of America's Future, 1584–2069*. Birth cohorts provide a popularly convenient way to categorize—for baby boomers, those born between World War II and Vietnam. As noted in the following chart, there was a population swell during this period after a lull between the Great Depression and up to World War II. This post war period in America saw a defining surge in births and also experienced a number of unique period events. While the popular understanding of cohorts has influenced religiosity study, this book will remain focused on more academic treatments of cohorts.

5. Herzog and Snell, "Youth and Emerging Adults"; Seversen, "Millennials Connecting to Contemporary Congregations"; Smith and Snell, *Souls in Transition*.

6. Richardson, *You Found Me*.

7. Putnam, *Bowling Alone*, 73.

8. Mills et al., "Listening and Enabling," 8.

outreach, drawing in spiritual done's who left the church in droves across previous generations?

Our rural churches tend to focus on two key ministry areas. First, we have a youth ministry, since that is considered to be the future of the church. Second, we care for the elderly shut-ins or those in need because it is the right thing to do. These ministries are amazing—but are they the only ministries that we should be considering as rural churches?

*Our desired identity drives ministry more than what our rural demographics tell us.*

Think about how many of the churches in your community host their own youth group, even if the public schools are consolidating due to a shrinking student population. Or, if your community is part of a sizable minority of rural areas that are burgeoning with an influx of young families, does it make sense that *every* church has a youth group? Is the drive for youth ministry due to perceived identity of a healthy church, or because of God's leading to meet a need in the community?

Likewise, when we think of the elderly, we automatically assume that it is a care ministry to those in need. Once again, this is very important—but are the only elderly in our rural communities those who are to be physically cared for? I would maintain that we need to drop our identity driven tools of focusing only on youth and certain segments of the elderly. There is a burgeoning group in many of our communities, and it constitutes what we often bemoan about our churches.

Dropping our tools might require us to reach out to the gray hairs of our rural community with intentionality. As much as we might complain about our church being mostly older adults, that just might be the demographic that rural churches are well suited to reach.

Again, baby boomers entering into early old age do not grab the headlines of concern nor of opportunity. Unless a baby boomer has aged prematurely and needs special assistance, very few churches view people entering into "early old age" to be a mission field brimming with opportunity. However, simply based on demographic shifts, as well as changes in religiosity that can take place with aging, those entering early old age should be of intentional ministry concern and focus for churches, especially rural churches.

## DEMOGRAPHIC SHIFT

Based on United States Census Bureau projections, older people will out-number children under the age of eighteen in the United States by the year 2034. This will be a first ever milestone in the history of the nation. A primary driver in that change is the large baby boomer generation (born 1946 to 1964) moving into retirement age.[9] The projected population change is daunting: the estimated senior population in 2016 was 49.2 million, but by 2034 that population is projected to be 77.0 million. Meanwhile, the eighteen and under population remains fairly steady, projected to only increase from 73.6 million to 76.5 million.[10]

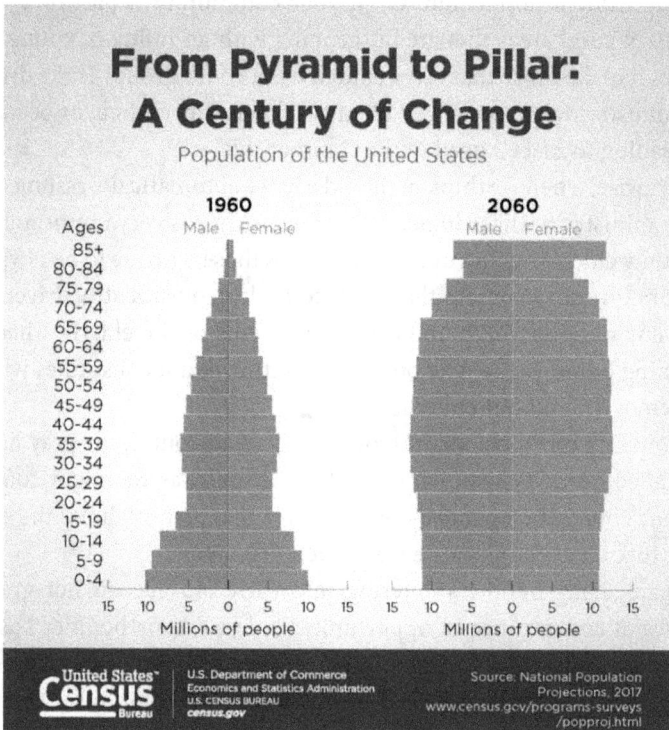

**U.S. Population Distribution by Age Shifts "From Pyramid to Pillar"**

No longer will there be the traditional pyramid of ages, in which there is a large foundation of children under the age of eighteen and a rapidly

9. United States Census Bureau, "2030 Marks Important Demographic Milestones."
10. United States Census Bureau, "Aging Nation."

dwindling pinnacle of seniors over the age of 65. By 2060, it is projected that there will be a pillar in which no single age demographic is exceptionally dominant.[11]

Geographic concentration of aging is especially evident in rural America. A full 85 percent of counties in the United States defined as "older-age counties" are rural. "Older-age counties" are where the sixty-five or older age bracket makes up at least 20 percent of the population—1,104 counties of the 3,141 counties in the United States meet this definition.[12] Coupled with this concentration of older-age counties, rural areas tend to be older on average. Statistics show 15 percent of the urban population in the United States is sixty-five or older while 19 percent of the rural population falls within that age bracket.[13]

## RELIGIOSITY[14]

Coupled with the increase in the number of adults over age sixty-five, there are indications of a rise in religious interest amongst baby boomers as they enter early old age.[15] Although there is not complete unanimity in opinion about age related change in religiosity, there is a general indication that self-identified religiosity increases with old age.[16] We will talk about this more later in the book, but we should first of all be clear by what we mean by "religiosity." The word sounds stuffy—but it opens the door to assessing faith commitment.

---

11. United States Census Bureau, "From Pyramid to Pillar." It is important to note that the United States is not leading this worldwide trend, but is mirroring a trend already underway. Japan's median age is already over 48 years old. By the year 2060, the Japanese government estimates that there will be one elderly person for every one working age person (IMF News 2020). The silver tsunami has already arrived in much of the world, pointing to implications of this research that reach beyond the borders of the United States.

12. United States Department of the Interior, "How Many Counties?" There are 3,141 counties or county equivalents in the United States—excluding territories.

13. United States Department of Agriculture, "Rural America at a Glance," 5.

14. One clear delimitation to take note of is that the qualitative research in the data sections of this book are specifically associated with the religiosity of Christians who attend conservative Protestant churches in the rural context of the North Central Region of the United States.

15. Silverstein and Bengtson, "Return to Religion?," 7, 13, 20.

16. Silverstein and Bengtson, "Return to Religion?," 8.

*Religiosity* is commonly measured using the framework of belonging, believing, and behaving.[17] Belonging is measured by variables such as church attendance.[18] Believing is measured by cognitive aspects such as self-identified beliefs, self-identified intensity of belief,[19] as well as assessments of adherence to traditional, orthodox Christian belief.[20] Behaving is measured by variables such as level of volunteering[21] and actions. Behaving through volunteering and life actions allow nonbelievers to "try out a Christian identity before committing to it."[22] Behaving can also be assessed through questions that identify components of the moral lifestyle of participants.[23]

## THE CHALLENGE OF THE "SILVER TSUNAMI"

There are twin factors presented to rural churches concerning baby boomers: 1) demographic shifts, and 2) religiosity increases connected to older age. The problem is that the demographic shift is often seen as a societal burden and the spiritual sensitivity has been largely unrecognized by the rural church. The demographic shift has earned the popular (though ageist) phraseology of "silver tsunami" where: the percentage of the population in the workforce declines, the increased demand for health services stretches the budgetary expense for Medicare, the increased pressure upon the Social Security program endangers its solvency, and social and policy changes are required to adapt transportation, buildings, and technology to the needs of an aging population.[24]

---

17. Olson and Warber, "Belonging, Behaving, and Believing," 192–204; Putnam and Campbell, *American Grace*; Seversen, "Millennials Connecting to Contemporary Congregations," 224.

18. Seversen, "Millennials Connecting to Contemporary Congregations," 224; Bengtson et al., "Does Religiousness Increase with Age?," 367; Hayward and Krause, "Aging, Social Developmental," 984.

19. Silverstein and Bengtson, "Return to Religion?," 11. Bengtson et al., "Does Religiousness Increase with Age?," 367; Hayward and Krause, "Aging, Social Developmental," 984.

20. Smith and Snell, *Souls in Transition*, 124, 135.

21. Silverstein and Bengtson, "Return to Religion?," 12.

22. Seversen, "Millennials Connecting to Contemporary Congregations," 231, 234.

23. Smith and Snell, *Souls in Transition*, 265–75.

24. Henderson et al., "Silver Tsunami," 153, 167.

Churches are not free from this attitude of seeing the elderly as a burden rather than a group of people with spiritual needs to be met, or who may even be able to make significant contributions to congregational life.[25] Less than one in five congregations have traditionally provided a program designed specifically for the elderly.[26] This measurement in and of itself is telling—counting the programs that serve the elderly, not involving the elderly in ministry. A compelling quote from Bengtson, et al. highlights the significance of this:

> There are 75 million baby boomers in this country, and half are now over the age of 60. Most are vibrant, healthy, they have more time in retirement to explore opportunities that give meaning to their lives. Many of these boomers had grown up in a church but had dropped out. So, what are churches today doing to attract these older adults, to meet their needs for spiritual growth and community? For the most part, nothing.[27]

The rising "silver tsunami" of retiring adults needs to be realized as a hopeful opportunity—a "potential mission field for organized religious bodies."[28] Given the demographic shift of aging and the possibility of increased religiosity in later life, there is an understudied opportunity for the rural church: baby boomers entering early old age. It is to the topic of aging that we now turn.

25. Rolph et al., "What Churches May Have to Learn," 60; Ramsey and Blieszner, *Spiritual Resiliency and Aging*. Rolph et al. develop these conclusions by drawing upon a report commissioned by the Centre for Policy on Ageing: Howse, *Religion, Spirituality, and Older People*.

26. Cnaan et al., "Religious Congregations as Social Services," 120. The Cnaan et al. study was of the Philadelphia area.

27. Bengtson et al., "Older Adults in Churches," 154.

28. Bengtson et al., "Older Adults in Churches," 176.

# CHAPTER 4

# Identity Shaped by Aging

W E are quick to jump to anecdotal evidence of age influences on a person's faith. Likewise, we have a proclivity in rural ministry to skip over theory that can inform our context-specific approach and delve right into application of what has worked in other locations. In this book, we are looking to move beyond anecdotal and look at some data to give us better ideas of where rural ministry can pick up some tools. In order to do this, we are going to walk through data-based literature that gives us a well-informed foundation to build from.

A quick disclaimer here: if theory is not your jam, do not give up on this book by reading this chapter. You can skim or skip this chapter and still soak in the rest of the book. If you have wondered about the theory behind religious change that comes with age, this is your chapter!

There are two main threads to the linkage of aging and religiosity: 1) the developmental process and 2) practical changes. Practical change refers to an individual's responses to losses that come with loneliness and changes in social networks, along with additional time that comes with retirement. Developmental changes refer to what takes place with an individual's ontogenetic, or individual developmental, progression. We will first examine the developmental process as described by Vern Bengtson and Merrill

Silverstein[1] which builds on the foundations of classic theorists such as Kohlberg,[2] Erikson,[3] and Tornstam.[4]

## DEVELOPMENTAL PROCESS

Bengtson and Silverstein utilized data from the Longitudinal Study of Generations (LSOG)[5] to conclude that while a majority of baby boomers remained stable in their religiosity over the previous ten years (51 percent) a significant minority (21 percent) did identify an increase in their religiosity.[6] Let's not skip over this quantitative finding too quickly—21 percent of a generation increasing in religiosity is a big deal, and is significant enough to better understand what is pushing baby boomers toward deeper faith.[7]

Based on their research, the developmental process was the primary motivation.[8] More specifically, "our results suggest that reasons for religious strengthening come primarily from internal processes such as spiritual desire, as well as religion's capacity to provide a sense of meaning beyond the material world, and serve as a psychic resource for coping with distressing life events."[9] Simply put, there is an age-related, internal, person

---

1. Bengtson et al., "Does Religiousness Increase with Age?," 363–79; Silverstein and Bengtson, "Return to Religion?," 7–21. Vern Bengtson, a social psychologist who held a PhD in human development and social psychology, was a long-term professor of gerontology, social work, and sociology at the University of Southern California. Merrill Silverstein often collaborated in research with Bengtson, and is the Marjorie Cantor Endowed Professor in Aging at Syracuse University.

2. "Stages and Aging in Moral Development," 497–502.

3. *The Life Cycle Completed.*

4. "Maturing into Gerotranscendence," 166–80.

5. Silverstein and Bengtson, "Return to Religion?," 7. Bengtson et al., "Does Religiousness Increase with Age?"

6. Silverstein and Bengtson, "Return to Religion?," 12.

7. Interestingly enough, Bengtson himself offers a glimpse at his personal interest in this subject through his own "return" in later life. He briefly chronicles his personal return to church attendance and involvement when he was nearly seventy years old (Bengtson 2013, xi).

8. Silverstein and Bengtson, "Return to Religion?," 18–19. The researchers utilized the 2016 wave of the LSOG, focusing on 599 respondents to look at religious change amongst baby boomers. Focusing on the group that increased in religiosity, quantitative and qualitative approaches led the researchers to conclude that both developmental changes and practical reasons have an impact on religious change. While noting practical influences, Bengtson and Silverstein focus on developmental process.

9. Silverstein and Bengtson, "Return to Religion?," 18.

specific push to reconsider religion.[10] While that statement can be simply put, we need to be aware that there is tremendous complexity that factors into the summary.[11] Yes, we are complicated—as evidenced by the push of practical changes.

## PRACTICAL CHANGES

Among researchers looking at the influence of aging on religiosity, there are also those who acknowledge the influence of developmental changes yet focus on changes in practical needs that take place due to the aging process. Hayward and Krause[12] represent researchers who are paying special

10. Bengtson et al., "Does Religiousness Increase with Age?," 266, 367, 371. This focus on religious change driven by developmental change brought on by aging builds on previous research that Bengtson and Silverstein were involved in. Their previous study utilized the LSOG, focused on the eight waves of the longitudinal study between 1970 and 2005, and involved 3,400 people from 420 multi-generational families, although it was focused in southern California. The researchers also utilized a qualitative study of twenty-five four-generational families, representing 157 members of the LSOG.

11. It is important to note that Bengtson and Silverstein enter into the debate surrounding age, period, and cohort (APC). They found that aging facilitates increasing religious expression of beliefs. Generation, or cohort, influences the perception of God as immanent and personal versus transcendent and sovereign. Cohort also influences the leaning toward organized religion or individual spirituality. Period effects such as economic recessions, wars, or social change are seen as potential influences. Bengtson et al., "Does Religiousness Increase with Age?," 363–66. Age, period, and cohort are collectively referred to as APC—three-time sensitive influences that are critical to assess when conducting aging research (Weil, *Research Design*, 26). APC analysis is a popular way to analyze large amounts of data (Fu, *Practical Guide*, 3) and its use reaches back to the 1860s (Fosse and Winship, "Analyzing Age-Period-Cohort Data," 468). Age is simply the time elapsed since a person was born. Period is the date of the study or observation. Cohort refers to the time span in which a person was born (Fu, *Practical Guide*, 3; Fosse and Winship, "Analyzing Age-Period-Cohort Data," 468; Riley, "On the Significance of Age in Sociology," 2; Weil, 26). We are looking at three main types of changes. First, how a person changes as they age. Second, how events in a particular year or a series of experiences impacted and shaped people who lived through that time. Third, how a group of people are unique because of the socialization processes they have experienced over their lives (Fosse and Winship, "Analyzing Age-Period-Cohort Data," 468). While Bengtson, Silverstein, and their colleagues found indications of aging, period, and cohort, their use of qualitative along with quantitative assessments led them to conclude that "it would appear that life course trajectories may trump generational placement as predictors of religious behaviors and orientations." Bengtson et al., "Does Religiousness Increase with Age?," 376.

12. R. David Hayward holds a PhD in social psychology and has served as a medical researcher for a variety of institutions. Neal Krause is Professor Emeritus of Health

attention to practical changes such as the need for emotional and tangible support in later life, and the impact that has on religious behavior.[13]

Practical changes do not influence religiosity separately from the developmental process yet do provide their own unique influences.[14] Hayward and Krause utilized data from the World Values Survey/European Values repeated cross-sectional study, which studied eighty nations across a thirty-two-year period. Of their conclusions, they found that aging was a significant factor in religious involvement. Interestingly enough however, the researchers maintain that "the relationship between religion and aging is widespread, but not universal."[15] Although there is a relationship between aging and religious involvement across cultures, there is significant variation in the strength of that relationship. For instance, "Western culture zones" tend to be especially strong in the aging-religious involvement connection.[16]

These differences point to the importance of social factors associated with aging, which can vary across cultures. While the developmental process is seen as a more universal phenomenon, the support offered by a religious body is much more culture specific. For instance, if a given locality has limited secular alternatives for support in older age, religious groups may see an appreciable increase in membership with aging because of prevalent unmet social needs.[17] There is also the practical possibility of more available time following retirement in later life which allows for greater corporate religious involvement.[18] The opportunity for churches to fill the void created by a lack of services is particularly applicable in some of our rural contexts—especially those communities that are seeing a rise in the early retiree population.

When specifically examining social support offered to aging adults by churches, Hayward and Krause found that emotional support from the

Behavior & Health Education at the University of Michigan School of Public Health and holds a PhD in sociology.

13. Hayward and Krause, "Patterns of Change"; Hayward and Krause, "Changes in Church-Based Social Support"; Hayward and Krause, "Aging, Social Developmental, and Cultural Factors."

14. Hayward and Krause, "Aging, Social Developmental, and Cultural Factors," 980–81; Hayward and Krause, "Patterns of Change," 1481, 1486.

15. Hayward and Krause, "Aging, Social Developmental, and Cultural Factors," 990.

16. Hayward and Krause, "Aging, Social Developmental, and Cultural Factors," 990.

17. Hayward and Krause, "Aging, Social Developmental, and Cultural Factors," 990.

18. Hayward and Krause, "Patterns of Change," 1486.

church tends to increase across older age, while tangible support tends to remain stable or decrease. This may reflect the fact that friends and family can more effectively meet the practical, tangible needs, while the church is better suited to meet emotional needs. This could also reflect the fact that those needing the most tangible assistance stopped attending at an earlier age due to health factors, so it is mainly the "hardy" who continue on with mainly emotional support.[19]

There are two key factors influencing aging individuals to turn to churches for social/emotional support: the frequency of their church attendance and the cohesiveness of the congregation. The more someone attends, the more likely they are to give and receive support. Likewise, the more cohesive the group, the more they share in group identity and purpose, then the more support is given and received between individuals.[20] Thus, we see influences surrounding social changes with the aging process. As there are increasing emotional needs with loss of loved ones, personal health, and career opportunities, there are opportunities for emotional support through increasing participation in a church.[21] This focus of the aging process sees increasing emotional support through relationships.[22]

## LIFESPAN THEORY

Lifespan Theory takes developmental processes and practical changes into account, and then moves a step further[23] Lifespan Theory moves beyond fixed-biological influences, and also takes cultural influences into

19. Hayward and Krause, "Changes in Church-Based Social Support," 94. Baltes is directly interacted in with this discussion, noting that Lifespan Theory points to the idea of compensating for losses that come with age through optimizing resources that are available. Hayward and Krause highlight the resource of social networks as something that aging individuals optimize.

20. Hayward and Krause, "Changes in Church-Based Social Support," 95.

21. Hayward and Krause, "Changes in Church-Based Social Support," 94. Dillon and Wink, *In the Course of a Lifetime*, 81.

22. Hayward and Krause, "Changes in Church-Based Social Support," 94. Hayward and Krause remain tentative in their conclusions due to the statistical difficulty of separating age, period, and cohort. Likewise, there is variability between individuals—there is not one single religious experience trajectory based on age. In the end, "the best conclusion is that there appears to be some evidence that some people may become more involved in religion as they grow older." (Hayward and Krause, "Religion, Health, and Aging," 254).

23. Baltes et al., "Life Span Theory in Developmental Psychology," 643.

account.[24] Rather than simply assessing biological changes that take place according to a time-dependent, universal schedule, there are also elements of psychological and social mechanisms that bring about adult development.[25] Do not miss the importance here—adults are constantly developing in dynamic ways—they are not stagnant.

We will examine the work of Paul B. Baltes[26] to better grasp the influence of Lifespan Theory on understanding how and why faith changes among adults.[27] One of the hallmarks of Baltes's approach is that development is life-long—that ontogenesis is not simply a childhood phenomenon but continues into old age. However, this lifelong process does not follow traditional development assumptions—it is multidirectional and full of adaptation to the context.[28]

Lifespan aging helps us understand the change in how resources are used as people age. There are three key goals that a person follows across their lifetime of development. In early life, an individual's resource capacity is mainly oriented toward *growth*—higher levels of functioning. As lifespan development continues, there is greater emphasis on *maintenance and resilience* —continuing a certain level of functioning or returning to a given level after a loss. Finally, there is *regulation of losses*—adapting to unavoidable losses to continue the highest level of functioning possible.[29] The recognition of regulating losses is presented as something of a corrective to a more Pollyanna view of growth and positive aging throughout life. There is opportunity for emotional/spiritual growth opportunities during old age, but that needs to be qualified. [30] There is a need to recognize that this is in

24. Baltes et al., "Life Span Theory in Developmental Psychology," 644.

25. Alwin, "Integrating Varieties of Life Course Concepts," 209. Baltes et al., "Life Span Theory in Developmental Psychology," 574; Baltes, "Theoretical Propositions." Duane Alwin is the McCourtney Professor of Sociology and Demography at Penn State University. He has the unique perspective of a PhD in sociology with an accompanying minor in educational psychology.

26. Paul B. Baltes was a professor of psychology at a variety of universities, and also served as Director at the Max Planck Institute for Human Development in Berlin, Germany.

27. Developmental theorists such as Erikson, Kohlberg, and Tornstam are included in the realm of lifespan approaches. Silverstein and Bengtson, "Return to Religion?," 9.

28. Baltes et al., "Life Span Theory in Developmental Psychology," 569; Baltes, "Theoretical Propositions," 611.

29. Baltes et al., "Life Span Theory in Developmental Psychology," 578.

30. Baltes presents the idea of "biocultural co-constructivism" to explain the intersection of individual development and period/cohort context. This intersection is composed

part compensation due to losses experienced in other areas of life.[31] The process can be incredibly painful and emotionally laden.

At this point, we can start seeing the opportunities that abound for the rural church. If we are intentionally reaching out to early old age adults, we are observant of their time in life in which they are bridging from a focus on *maintenance and resilience* to a *regulation of losses*. There is a different mindset that people are working from that we need to be aware of.

Lifespan Theory goes on to offer us a more specific understanding of how this works—the more specific aging process of "selective optimization with compensation" (SOC). Here is how it works. When a person thinks about the good stuff of life, they select life outcome goals that move them toward their desired experiences. These aspirations might be a vacation home on the lake or extended travel. But, life is not all rainbows and puppy dogs.

SOC also recognizes that aging individuals face the junk of life. Over the course of time, individuals also select some loss-based goals to get through negative life experiences. No longer are they focused on aspirations, they have moved to avoidance of the worst outcomes. The individual optimizes their resources as much as possible or compensates for the loss of resources that they were forced to accept.[32] Hence, aging individuals exhibit

---

of three main paths. There are age-graded influences that are generally normative across individuals. There are history-graded influences which impact an individual's development. Finally, there are non-normative influences. There are unique experiences of the individual that shape their development, such as the loss of a limb—something that is not predictable and presents a definitive life challenge (Baltes et al., "Life Span Theory," 587–88). The tension of age-graded and history-graded impact of period can be seen in current debate surrounding the impact of COVID-19. There are those who side with history-graded and strongly caution against too much attention being given to cohort specific impact through highlighting presumed generational differences in impact (Rudolph and Zacher, "COVID-19 Generation," 139–45). This is counter to age-graded catch phrases surrounding COVID-19 that are harshly tweeted, memed, and then mentioned in popular media, such as "boomer remover" (Whalen, "What Is 'Boomer Remover?'"). Likewise, age-graded advocates see specific baby boomer specific changes in retirement experience/expectations compared to other generations (Novack, "8 Ways Coronavirus"; Tergesen, "How Covid-19 Will Change").

31. Baltes et al., "Life Span Theory," 579.

32. Baltes et al., "Life Span Theory," 594. Utilizing SOC, the individual selects growth goals—positive results they desire through experiences. The individual also pursues a regulation of losses, they attempt to minimize the cost of negative change that their context or life change hands them. Growth goals are aimed at aspirations while the regulation of losses is focused on avoidance. As a person ages and there is a rise in losses compared to growth opportunities, there is a focus on maintenance and resilience— continuing a

plasticity in how they handle the good and bad with aging. There are many commonalities among aging individuals based on developmental processes and practical needs, but there is also inter-individual variability and intra-individual difference.[33] Weighing out how to maximize the good and contain the bad situations in life is what we all do—but it looks different for different people and it might be different for each one of us depending on the day.

The idea of plasticity, that individuals change how they think with a change in circumstances, highlights the "adaptive capacity" that we have as we age. Individuals themselves proactively shape their later in life development through how they respond to life events.[34] Aging impacts the blend of gains and losses that an individual faces, but there is not a simple biologically determined response, nor is there complete arbitrariness to the response. People seek out options for positive gains even in the face of unavoidable losses. This means that significant late life changes happen—early life experiences influence but do not predetermine how people necessarily experience later life.[35] This is critical to remember as we think about faith changes that can come with aging. People are not simply set in their ways.

Let's take SOC a step further and examine how gains and losses impact a person's socioemotional goals as they age.[36] Just what we all want, another theory with an acronym. Socioemotional selectivity theory (SST) posits that the shrinking of social networks as people age is not an unwanted reality, but an example of selective optimization with compensation (SOC) where emotional well-being is the goal. The reduction of relationships with aging

---

certain level of functioning or returning to a given level after a loss (Baltes et al., "Life Span Theory," 578). This is very much a rational choice decision making process at play—the individual optimizes their resources as much as possible or compensates for the loss of resources that they were forced to accept (Baltes et al., "Life Span Theory," 594).

33. Baltes et al., "Life Span Theory," 621.

34. Baltes et al., "Life Span Theory," 582.

35. Baltes et al., "Life Span Theory," 584.

36. Baltes and Carstensen, "Process of Successful Ageing," 409, 411, 413; English and Carstensen, "Selective Narrowing of Social Networks," 201. Laura L. Carstensen is the founding director of the Stanford Center on Longevity. The Center on Longevity also collaborates with the Carstensen Life-span Development Laboratory which "focuses on the social, emotional, and cognitive processes that people use to adapt to life circumstances as they age." Carstensen received her PhD from West Virginia University in clinical psychology and currently serves as Professor of Psychology and the Fairleigh S. Dickinson Jr. Professor in Public Policy at Stanford University (https://longevity.stanford.edu/people-2/laura-carstensen/).

mainly involves peripheral connections, while close relationships remain stable. This coincides with "growing evidence that, on balance, emotional experience grows more positive with age."[37] Hence, aging-related goals, not just limitations, shape the social context that the early old age function within.[38]

## APPLICATION

This discussion of age has indicated the value of utilizing multiple vantage points when assessing changes in religiosity. When it comes to the influence of the aging process, we have observed that there are: 1) developmental influences, 2) practical influences such as desire for social support, 3) socially shaped aging influences ascribed by roles and expectations, and 4) possibilities for an individual to intentionally select late in life changes in religiosity.

We now have a foundation to build from to examine the tools necessary for reaching adults in our rural communities, especially those entering into early old age. Much of the data presented in this chapter is based on quantitative research that is incredibly valuable for knowing where to begin. In order to better grasp how to practically reach people in our rural communities though, we now turn to qualitative research that provides richer, fuller data.

37. English and Carstensen, "Selective Narrowing of Social Networks," 195, 200. Carstensen, *Long, Bright Future*. English and Carstensen make the important note that the emotional improvements that grow with age are not all related to changes in social networks through socioemotional selectivity theory. It is one example of how the broader theory of selective optimization with compensation impacts the age-related goal of emotional regulation and overall improvement.

38. Yet, socioemotional aging is not simply a matter of agency, but the culture(s) that the person lives in across their lifespan shape(s) their expectations of what emotional well-being looks like and feels like. Fung, "Aging in Culture," 375.

# CHAPTER 5

# Qualitative Data

T HE qualitative research undertaken for this book included an investigation of baby boomers who self-identify as increasing in Christian religiosity. A primary concern was to listen for how they described their own change from a place of no faith or nominal faith to what they consider to be a devout Christian. The research specifically focused on how their religiosity changed as they entered early old age in the rural American context.

## RESEARCH BASIS

The data utilized by this book builds from research that involved fifty qualitative interviews, including thirty-one baby boomer interviews and nineteen pastor or ministry leader interviews. Gender representation of the baby boomer interviews included seventeen female and fourteen male. There were twenty-eight different churches represented in the interviews, connected with nine different denominations, conferences, or independent church status. A variety of church sizes were represented as well, ranging from an average attendance of a house church of less than ten people to a congregation of over three-hundred fifty people.[1]

Baby boomer informants met the following criteria: 1) member of the baby boomer cohort (born 1946–1964); 2) self-identifies as a Christian who has increased in religiosity (belonging, believing, behaving) in the

1. This research built from a previous qualitative study conducted by the author involving a single Conference of churches where there were 2 focus groups, 11 site observations, and 23 personal interviews.

past ten years, 3) self-identifies their starting point as a place of no faith or nominal faith; 4) is connected to a conservative Protestant church or ministry; 5) residential context is outside the most metropolitan areas as designated by the USDA ERS Rural Urban Continuum Code (RUCC) in the North Central Region of the United States.

Pastors and ministry leaders met the following criteria: 1) serve as the lead pastor of a church or lead a ministry initiative; 2) serve with a conservative Protestant church or ministry; 3) have significant interaction with baby boomers in ministry; 4) pastoral context is outside the most metropolitan areas as designated by the USDA ERS Rural Urban Continuum Code (RUCC) in the North Central Region of the United States.

As we will see more clearly in future chapters, careful listening and semi-structured prompting are especially important for faith stories to be shared by those entering early old age. We often do not consider the challenges that people face as they age and are called on to share their story. One group of researchers state:

> Little is written of the inherent practical difficulties in questioning and listening to older people speaking about sensitive issues. For some older people, such matters can include personal beliefs, which may never have been readily discussed before. We also have to bear in mind that thoughts about beliefs and values may never have been fully processed and thus remain difficult to articulate. The older person may fear being judged as foolish, uneducated, or misunderstood.[2]

People entering early old age are especially vulnerable to the social pressure of 'having life figured out' due to their extensive life experiences. Having a safe space where their stories can still have loose ends is very important, and storytelling opportunities are essential for people to work through some of their questions that arise with aging. And as we will see, based on people's stories, there are a number of factors associated with aging.

2. Mills et al., "Listening and Enabling," 35.

# AGING INFLUENCES IDENTIFIED THROUGH QUALITATIVE RESEARCH

Baby boomers circled around three main aging elements: gains, losses, and identity.[3] Reflecting Baltes' observation of selective optimization with compensation, baby boomers look at these three elements in balancing maintenance, resilience, and regulation of losses. The storyteller would tend to walk through gains that they have enjoyed during early old age and share how that has impacted their religiosity. There was also a significant focus on losses, where there have been difficult changes in early old age, or changes across the lifespan that have a cumulative impact in early old age.

Finally, there was also a theme of identity that emerged—baby boomers shared a change in values with aging. There was a cluster of items in many baby boomers' stories that demonstrated a shift in what matters to them compared to earlier in life. We turn first to the gains that baby boomers referenced in their stories.

## GAINS

Gains refer to the positive experiences that baby boomers have soaked in during their transition into early old age. Most of the positive aspects surround free time and change in the priority of work, the flexibility of work, or even the experience of the legacy of their work. There was also an important element of relationships included in the gains that indicated change.

### Retirement

Just over half of the participants identified as retired, seventeen out of thirty-one. The number of retired roughly reflects the age spectrum of baby boomers, where the older wave has largely moved into retirement while the

---

3. Biological influences shared by baby boomers included their own health, illness of others, and death of a loved one. Developmental influences included changes in the nature of their work—from retirement to part-time work to more flexible schedules. Another developmental shift included the change in roles with aging parents, children, and grandchildren. Practical influences included caregiving responsibilities for those aging parents, young grandchildren, and children who are in times of transition. Other practical influences involved opportunities to engage in community volunteering or mission-oriented work. Social influences included the elevated importance of certain relationships while other relationships faded, such as those at a previous place of work.

younger wave is still gainfully employed. Stories of the seventeen who are retired pointed to a perceived increase in religiosity due to the additional time and release from the emotional and psychological strain associated with work life.[4]

When it comes to the significance of retirement, many referenced the blessing of free time to do what they enjoy. There were stories about increased travel, picking up a hobby, moving to their vacation home for full time residence, and controlling their own schedule. When it came to change in religiosity, many indicated that retirement allows for an increase in time for participation in church and practice of spiritual disciplines. Thomas said that he "was never one to get into Bible studies or anything" even though it "would have helped." He simply never made the time for "study and meeting other people" until he "retired from work."

The increase in belonging through small group participation was evident among these seventeen, where fourteen of the seventeen noted an increase in the importance or consistency of their small group engagement. The increase in volunteering was likewise noticeable, where 83 percent of baby boomers who are retired or work part-time shared stories about the significance of volunteering, while only 25 percent of those who did not identify with retirement shared a similar story.

But when it comes to practicing spiritual disciplines, baby boomers did not tend to provide the same connection between retirement and increasing importance or practice. While many mentioned the additional time to do so, only nine of the seventeen who retired spoke of an increase in actually practicing prayer differently. That means that 53 percent of those who retired spoke of an increase in the practice of prayer, while 79 percent of those not retired expressed a moderate to significant change in prayer. This indicates that the increase in available time for spiritual disciplines may be neutralized by the loss of structure to the day.

It is important to note the new cultural phenomenon that we are assessing here. While retirement has existed for years, baby boomers are experiencing something new as they largely retire with years of good health still

---

4. There is some variation in how baby boomers are embracing retirement. Of the seventeen who consider themselves retired, six referred to transitioning into part-time work which carried different levels of responsibility and stress. In addition, there were six individuals who did not refer to retirement, but discussed their transition to part-time work. This group of six noted the increase in free time, but continue to find significant identity in their work and see this as a continuation of their work life trajectory rather than a significant change.

ahead of them. This elevates the potential for gains during this time of life compared to previous generations, and also has implications for churches to consider as they look for opportunities to connect with people entering early old age. Increase in small group attendance as well as volunteering reveals that baby boomers have a desire for ministry "with" in early old age rather than the traditional assumption that ministry for retired adults is only "to them" and need-based.

## Retirement Correlation with Volunteering And Inverse Correlation with Prayer

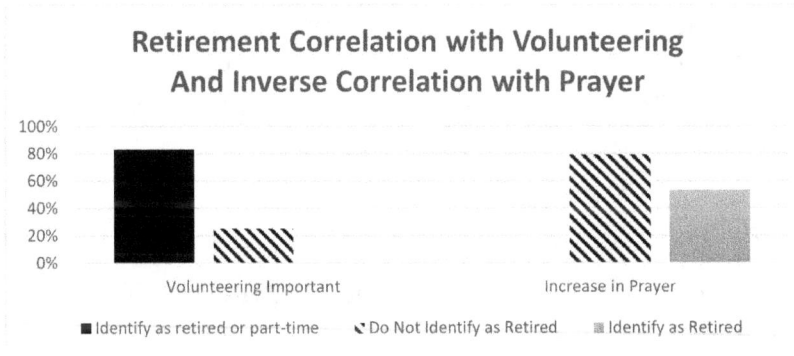

Retirement Correlation with Volunteering and Inverse Correlation with Prayer

## Flexibility and Legacy

Regardless of whether or not baby boomers were retired, flexibility in life and a sense of work legacy play an important role in the gains experienced at early old age. Flexibility in life refers to the ability to have a malleable schedule where routine demands are lessened. Some described this as an increase in flexibility when it comes to their work schedules—even those still working talked about the perks of seniority. Many spoke of the flexibility that comes with not having children in the home while others spoke of not feeling the need to be involved in as many civic functions to build their relationship base.

Don talked about the increased amount of time that was freed up in his schedule when he no longer held a lead role in the local Chamber of Commerce. He had enjoyed the Chamber for the relationships it provided, but he found the leadership role to be relationally draining and very time consuming. Overall, twenty-eight spoke of an increase in flexibility, and twenty-seven shared stories indicating a sense of work legacy over their life span. Work legacy is a sense of pride and accomplishment through one's employment and a sense that current achievement is not as necessary because of security through what has already been recognized in one's work.

While flexibility or work legacy were mentioned by all thirty-one participants, these were a soft, or indirect influence on religiosity. Some mentioned that flexibility made it easier to be involved in church activities, but this seemed to be more of a passing reference, unlike the impact of retirement. No one talking about work legacy mentioned that this directly impacted their believing, belonging, or behaving. Indirectly, the release from some of the emotional and psychological pressures of work and life in general were referenced in these conversations, but not directly impacting their faith journey.

## Relationships

All thirty-one participants shared that relationships had an increasing role in their lives over the past ten years. Most shared stories of a decrease in quantity of relationships coupled with a rise in quality of relationships, especially among those who had retired. People who had relocated within the past ten years spoke of dramatic changes in relationships. Yet, amidst this change, there was an underlying sentiment that baby boomers were finding relationships that mattered in early old age. The qualitative interviews clearly highlighted Carstensen's socioemotional selectivity theory—fewer but highly valued relationships of depth.

Thomas spoke about how his siblings had become more connected despite geographic distance as they entered early old age. The four siblings all increased in the amount that they communicated and also the depth of their communication—where faith was becoming a more significant topic of conversation even though one of the four was a long-term agnostic. Becky shared how her sister and brother-in-law intervened in her life during a time of manic mental illness—an intervention that she speculates would not have taken place prior to early old age when their relationship became deep enough to withstand the strain.

Harold represented many when he talked about his work relationships after his retirement. Since he no longer had contact with people on a daily basis, many of the friendships faded to more of acquaintances. Yet, the handful of closest friendships that he developed at work continued and deepened. These friends continue contact by text and phone, along with occasional gatherings at a restaurant or golf course. These friendships have moved deeper as one of the friends has struggled with cancer, and conversations moved to spiritual topics that had not been broached before.

As we will see, there are also plenty of examples of negative changes in certain relationships, but as a matter of overall aging, this group expressed a winnowing of relationships as a positive experience. The narrowing of relationships has been coupled with a time of deepening friendships and significant conversations. While relationships are a significant positive aging experience, its impact on religiosity seems to be more indirect. The changing nature of relationships reflects the overall desire for belonging but does not necessitate a desire for belonging to a church or para-church group.

## Summary of Gains

The impact of relationships is indicative of the broad category of age-related gains overall—wide swaths of baby boomers are experiencing gains as they enter early old age, but the direct impact on elements of faith seems to be limited. The limited positive impact of gains on religiosity was echoed through pastor interviews. Pastors noted the additional time where baby boomers *could* choose to invest more in believing, belonging, and behaving. However, pastors emphasized the disruptions created by gains that do not facilitate growth in religiosity. For instance, a number of pastors mentioned how many baby boomers became sporadic in participation after retirement. Pastors from more rural areas noted the travel to visit children and grandchildren who are at a distance. Pastors in less rural areas noted the summer camps and seasonal use of cottages that many escape to during good weather (and rural pastors in amenity rich areas noted the swell of vacationing attenders in summer). Regardless of the rurality, pastors mentioned the impact of snowbirds.

Baby boomers indicated that gains contribute to change of religiosity through indirect channels. Pastors of baby boomers noted that the contribution of gains to change in religiosity was limited by competing priorities. As we turn to age-related losses, we will observe how fewer baby boomers are impacted by each category, but the direct impact on religiosity is more observable.

## Losses

Aging brings on two felt influences of losses. First, the sheer volume of losses through death, illness, and the like increase as people enter into early old age. Second, losses have added impact because they have been compounded over the life span. This second point is important to elaborate on as we enter into the discussion of losses.

When it comes to losses expressed by baby boomers, it can be difficult to categorize them while respecting the life span nature of losses. For instance, death and illness of a loved one during early old age might have greater significance due to an unresolved experience from earlier in life. The death of a sibling may have even more significance because it compounds the unresolved loss of a parent a decade earlier. When examining losses through the narrative accounts, I have done my best to bring in the life span importance of events and not simply look at the event through the lens of a single loss. At the same time, this view is only possible if the baby boomer looks at their own life story in this way.

We will now look at five losses that emerged as significant themes in a number of stories: 1) death of a loved one, 2) divorce, 3) illness of others, 4) personal loss of health, and 5) care giving. As we will see, the impact of losses on religiosity is more direct and observable than the influence of age-related gains.

### Death

Stories indicating that religiosity was changed due to the loss of a loved one were shared by 18 of the 31 participants. The most impactful stories surrounding death were not just a retelling of what happened a few years ago, but the choice of verb tense made it clear that many of these baby boomers are still being deeply impacted by these losses. Tanya told about the tragic death of her son due to suicide. She started the story by showing me a picture of her son during our Zoom interview. She wanted me to see as well as hear her stories of healthy pride that she had and continues to have for her son, an "amazing, amazing child" who was "the kindest, gentlest, giving person."

The death of Tanya's son brought about intense questions of "why." She can now see the series of events that led to her son's death, but that did not lead to deeper religiosity in and of itself. Through this intense time of grief, she found that she was not able to shoulder this experience alone, and that she needed to let her other children into vulnerable places in her life. With time, one of her daughters introduced her to a small group where she was able to soak in encouragement and make connections between Scripture and her felt life experiences.

This story of loss is reflective of an overall experience of others as well: fifteen of the eighteen who noted the spiritual significance of the death of loved ones also shared that they became increasingly engaged in a small group or attended for the first time. Only two people who experienced the death of a loved one found a sense of belonging through the worship service, not through participating in a small group.

There are a few other interesting sidebars when it comes to this group experiencing loss. Women seemed to be the most impacted through this form of loss. Many of the women mentioned their unique role as mom if the story included the loss of a child. Others discussed caregiving for elderly parents or in-laws as something of an expected gender role. In addition, multiple women had maintained careers in the medical or caregiving fields. All told, it is noteworthy that women were significantly impacted by this particular loss.

There is another group especially spiritually sensitive following the death of a loved one—those who have been least connected to a church. 92 percent of those who have been especially distanced from church experiences were impacted by the death of a loved one, while only 31 percent of those more connected to churches over their lifetime were impacted. The implications are significant. The death of a loved one for those who are deeply rooted in church experience is unlikely to create much movement in religiosity. On the other hand, those who grew up without a significant church experience are likely to be spurred to consider their faith. The specific audience being reached at a funeral service is worthwhile to consider.

This time of loss created a burst of activity in small group participation and volunteering, but it did not translate to long-term belonging on its own. Volunteering and small group opportunities are helpful to the baby boomer in a time of loss, but do not fill the void of long-term belonging. Hence, death should be seen as a window of opportunity for the church to engage in the lives of spiritually sensitive adults, but more than a grief group or community cleanup project is required to move to a place of faith engagement.

*Divorce*

Participants shared a variety of stories involving the loss of relationships, but one specific relationship change that was linked with faith stories involved divorce. The divorces did not necessarily happen within the past ten years, but the effects made an impact on the faith of the baby boomer during the last decade. Nine participants shared stories of divorce that impacted their faith—more may have been divorced, but they did not think that part of their life story has had an impact over the past years of change in faith. Of the nine, one shared how the divorce negatively impacted their faith, one shared that it made very little difference, three shared stories of moderate significance, and four shared stories of dramatic impact on their religiosity.

The group was not evenly dispersed among genders: six women shared stories of divorce, while only three men did so. Regardless of gender, there were connections with aspects of religiosity. All nine shared that some aspect of their moral behavior changed through the experience. All nine also mentioned that their participation in small groups was noticeably different following their divorce. The need for support and encouragement in a safe place was high enough that they were willing to engage with vulnerability.

Most of the stories involved marital counseling over an extended period of time prior to the divorce. Multiple stories involved marital infidelity on the part of the spouse. The combination of a herculean effort to save the marriage coupled with abject betrayal created a sense of "devastation" for a majority of those interviewed, including Betty. The divorce of Betty's parents left a deep scar on her life, and she vowed that she "was going to do marriage differently." She married with high hopes that making her "home a priority" would lead to a happy, long-lasting marriage. However, her husband cheated on her multiple times; they would separate and then get back together again. After trying to hold things together for years, Betty and her husband ended their marriage.

As Betty replayed her painful experience, she began to move away from placing all the blame on her husband and began to acknowledge that she had devoted herself "to the kids and not to the marriage." The cumulative experience of emotional exhaustion, betrayal, guilt, and the loss of the dream for a happy home led Betty to reach out to a sibling for support. The support that came was not only in the form of emotional support, but also included an invitation to join a small group Bible Study. As painful as the divorce was, it has served as a shaper of Betty's religiosity.

While divorce did not directly influence a large number of participants' stories, it had a deep impact where it was felt. Likewise, divorce serves as a representative of other types of loss in relationship that people are likely to experience over their life span. Difficult relationship loss such as divorce was linked to a change in elements of belonging (small groups) and behaving (lifestyle) by the baby boomers interviewed.

## Illness of Others

Twenty-one participants referenced the spiritually significant stories of illness that involved a friend or family member. Lorraine told the story of her mother's illness and the profound impact it had on her spiritual life. She and her mother had a long-term estranged relationship, but as her mother's illness progressed, the need to reconnect became more pronounced. The daughter was not only concerned about the relationship between her and her mother, but she also began to wonder about her mother's destination for eternity. The concern for her mother led to a great deal of introspection about her own standing with God and what her own life looked like. As the illness progressed, Lorraine talked about faith with her mother as she had never done previously in their lives. While her primary motivation was to ensure that her mother "went to heaven," a corollary was that she herself was changed. One significant change involved prayer, and this is a change representative of the group impacted by the illness of another.

The link between prayer and illness is intuitive—if someone we love is sick, we are likely to rely more on prayer. What is of interest is that stories shared did not simply indicate praying more, there was a change in the nature of their prayer. Most of this group were familiar with praying when things were difficult. Many times in life they had prayed for God to fix the problem, and then as the difficulty faded, they went back to life as usual. In early old age, rather than simply praying for things to be fixed according to their therapeutic desires, there was now more attention paid to God as sovereign—akin to the theme of "Thy will be done." Indeed, 80 percent of those who noted a change in their prayer life were also impacted by the illness of another. Looking at it from another angle, only 24 percent of those who shared a story of the illness of another did not share a story about the change in their prayer life.

Illness appears to be connected to the level of rurality as well. Those in the most rural areas were far and away the most likely to share stories about the impact of illness. Those in the most rural zones spoke about the distance to high quality health care for specific needs, as well as the dearth of mental health resources available to them. There was a perception that illness brought a great price: long distance travel for treatment, the need for people to rely on to obtain services, the labyrinth of referrals that might be required, and also the possibility that needed services would not be accessible.

Pastor Nick shared the story of a parishioner who erupted in the presence of medical personnel determining where to send an ill person. The medical team was leaning toward sending the person to a local hospital rather than the long-distance specialized care hospital. The parishioner begged them not to send their loved one to the local hospital because that was just an indication that they needed to go somewhere to die rather than to be treated. For those in the most rural areas, illness bore a different weight and significance in their stories compared to where medical care facilities were more local. This is a difference felt in personal loss of health as well.

### Personal Loss of Health

Stories that expressed loss of personal health as a cause for change in religiosity were shared by thirteen individuals. The stories ranged from long term issues that led to the amputation of a limb to an intense season of cancer treatment. While some stories detailed how their faith grew through slow recovery, the majority were impacted by a dramatic improvement in health or sense of God's manifest presence with them during a critical time.

Many shared stories of power encounters with God in which they were shaped by what they describe as a tangible experience with God. Gwen passionately shared her story of being declared clinically dead by the medical team working on her. While she was clinically dead, she experienced God's presence and heard His voice in a miraculous way. During this experience, God told her to share her story with others and to pray with them. Since that time, Gwen shares that her commitment to Jesus Christ has dramatically changed, and her talking about Jesus has moved from rarely to consistently.

Gwen's story points to another interesting connection—the group of people who told stories of health-related change in religiosity also shared specific stories about change in their lifestyle. Of the thirteen people with health-related stories, ten also shared their change in religiosity as a change in lifestyle. Gwen changed how expressive she is about her faith in public. She also spoke of how God got her attention to move away from bad habits in her life through power encounters. Sam related how he vowed that he would change certain behaviors that he knew were wrong if he came through a surgery. Although the change in health was cited by just over 40 percent of all participants, the impact was deeply felt based on the stories shared.

One final caveat leads us back to considering the potential influence of rurality on this variable. Over one-half of the participants in the most rural zones shared stories about personal health while only one-quarter of those in the least rural areas shared such stories. Based on the stories shared, the most probable cause is similar to the discussion regarding illness—the more removed the person is from a robust health care system, the greater the impact of health-related issues. We will see the impact of the rural zones once again as we examine the caregiving role in which baby boomers find themselves.

## Caregiving

Caregiving refers to significant assistance provided by the baby boomers to family members. Caregiving was extended to aging parents: transportation, housekeeping, medicine administration, admittance to a care facility, or providing care in one's own home. Caregiving was also extended to grandchildren: transportation, daycare provision, surrogate parenting, or guardianship. In some cases, caregiving was provided to adult children who had landed in a difficult place in life through drug addiction, mental illness, job loss, or divorce.

Caregiving was categorized as a loss because of how the stories were shared. Many participants were positive about the experience to be able to help, but there was an undertone that they would not choose the cost of this role. Caregiving carries a cost in terms of time and resources that are required because a family member has experienced a loss. Even when it comes to grandchildren, the caregiving role was taken because there is a loss that requires the grandparent to step in through a significant investment.

The caregiving role is also defined by a sense of life season. Betty shared about the stressful time when her daughter went through a difficult divorce with children, ages three and eight. Betty became involved as primary caregiver for the grandchildren during this season. As time went on though, the role as caregiver diminished to the point where Betty's daughter needed to say she was the parent and that she needed Betty "to back off some." The caregiving role was intense and had a significant impact on Betty's religiosity but was also for a specific season.

Over one-half of the participants, sixteen in total, cited a caregiving role and its impact on their religiosity. Gwen shared about the financial strain that she has been placed under as her children and grandchildren have gone for extended times without jobs. Despite this strain that went beyond her control, she has found solace in answered prayer surrounding provision.

Similar to divorce and death, there was a noticeable rise in belonging through small group participation. 94 percent of baby boomers who shared caregiving stories also noted moderate to significant increases in small group participation, while 63 percent of those not sharing caregiving stories mentioned a rise in small group impact.

Caregiving was also influenced by the rurality of the baby boomer. The distribution by rurality is quite telling: 83 percent of baby boomers in the least rural zones talked about caregiving but only 32 percent of those in other zones did so. When examining the stories of these baby boomers, only one of the six who shared stories in the most rural and moderately rural zones spoke of children or grandchildren, the other five cared for elderly parents or loved ones. On the other hand, six of the ten in the least rural zones spoke of caregiving for children or grandchildren, and only four spoke of caring for elderly parents as their primary caregiving experience.

For most baby boomers in the more rural areas, their children and grandchildren live at a distance and there is not the option of caregiving on a consistent basis. Many of the more rural areas have been impacted by the younger generation moving away for work. The least rural zones have enough proximity to urban areas where there has been sufficient work and cultural amenities to keep adult children and grandchildren in the area. A significant number of baby boomers have also moved to a more rural area upon their retirement that created or maintained a geographic distance between themselves and their children or grandchildren. Only one baby boomer spoke of intentionally moving to a more rural area to be closer to grandchildren. One qualifier on the correlation between rural zone and caregiving—there is also a gender disparity.

Only five of the sixteen who shared stories about caregiving are men. This most likely reflects some assumed gender roles for this cohort and also indicates the more significant impact that caregiving had on women compared to men.

One final caveat is that caregiving tended to make participants introspective about their own future, even if they have been experiencing good health. As Thomas shared about his own "very good health" in comparison to someone he provides care for, he notes that "someday when something lands" on him, he will "not like it very much." While baby boomers were seeking out support and encouragement through small groups during intense caregiving seasons, there also tended to be an increasing realization of their own mortality and finite future.

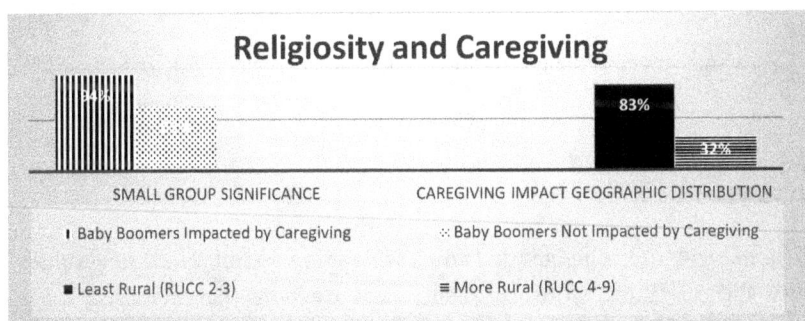

**Religiosity and Caregiving**

| | |
|---|---|
| SMALL GROUP SIGNIFICANCE | CAREGIVING IMPACT GEOGRAPHIC DISTRIBUTION |
| I Baby Boomers Impacted by Caregiving | ∴ Baby Boomers Not Impacted by Caregiving |
| ■ Least Rural (RUCC 2-3) | ≡ More Rural (RUCC 4-9) |

83%

Religiosity and Caregiving Linked with Small Groups and Geography

## Summary of Losses

While gains tended to be more indirect in their shaping of believing, belonging, and behaving, the role of losses influencing religiosity tended to be very visible and direct in the stories shared by baby boomers. Interviews with pastors of baby boomers highlighted the role of losses in catalyzing direct change of religiosity. Moving from this direct connection, we will go on to another more indirect aging influence, the role of identity.

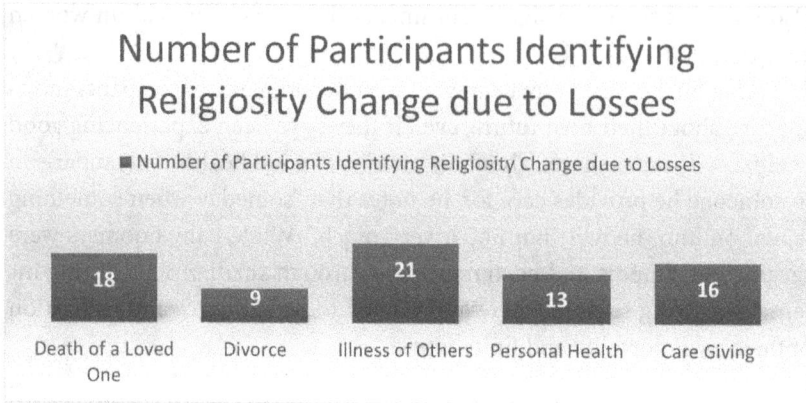

## Number of Participants Identifying Religiosity Change due to Losses

■ Number of Participants Identifying Religiosity Change due to Losses

| Death of a Loved One | Divorce | Illness of Others | Personal Health | Care Giving |
|---|---|---|---|---|
| 18 | 9 | 21 | 13 | 16 |

Number of Participants Identifying Religiosity Change Due to Losses

## IDENTITY

Religiosity identity changes that come with aging do not reflect new values, but a shift in values. More accurately, these are items that increased in priority on the value chain for baby boomers as they aged into early old age. Patty is representative of most of the baby boomers through her sharing about identity. She found that two significant changes took place as she entered into early old age. First, she began defining her identity less and less based on career and status as she elevated the importance of long-lasting spiritual matters. The spiritual matters were not sudden, new revelations— but they became more central and significant to her identity. Second, as Patty looked back over her life in early old age, she recognized that she had been so consumed by her own priorities earlier in life that she had missed engaging in the things that she wants people to remember about her. She has an increasing interest in her personal legacy.

We will take up these two changes in identity by looking at some specific themes. First, we will examine the general rise of interest in spiritual matters, along with a specific assessment of changes taking place in baby boomer participation in service opportunities that involve faith communication. Second, we will consider the stories shared about the rise of life review and concern for personal legacy, including specific references to children and grandchildren.

## Spiritual Interests Increase

Patty feels that her identity has shifted due to an increase in spiritual interests. She states that it was a "radical shift" to go from defining who she was by "earthly relationships, earthly status, titles, [and] job" to what she believes her identity truly is, "a child of God." She became more concerned about spiritual matters as they became central to her primary sense of identity. She increasingly saw spiritual matters as a key part of who she is, not simply what she uses as a coping mechanism. In other words, religious believing, belonging, and behaving became core elements of who she wanted to be, not simply to get what she wanted.

Of the thirty-one participants, twenty-nine shared stories indicating a moderate to significant rise in spiritual interests over the past ten years. When baby boomers talked about their shift in identity, they clearly referenced a change in their value chain. By the time they were reaching early old age, even those who had started life with a religious indifferent or actively nonreligious childhood had been religiously socialized to some degree. The baby boomers in this study had some semblance of spiritual values—but these values were generally latent or were used for therapeutic purposes. 94 percent of the baby boomers in this study indicated that the prioritizing of spiritual values came about, in part, because aging raised their awareness of the things in life that are passing and the things that are of eternal value.

Baby boomers did not only share this identity shift in conceptual terms—they also offered stories about tangible changes in their actions. Twenty-seven of the thirty-one baby boomers shared stories that demonstrated a change in priorities through their involvement in community ministry or mission work outside their own community. Community ministry included housing rehabilitation, food closets, and civic engagement—but all providing an opportunity to ultimately share one's faith with others. Mission activity had a variety of service elements involved, but once again focused on the opportunity to share one's faith as a significant corollary to the work.

Looking at the breakdown more specifically, we observe similarities between these two service areas: nineteen shared stories of change through community ministry and eighteen shared stories of change through mission work. Once again, the link between this service work and identity is that the goal is to do more than a good civic work; it is framed by living out one's faith and sharing that faith with others.

The increase in willingness to share one's faith story was mentioned by many as evidence of a change in identity. Most had been religiously socialized in a setting in which faith was a private matter, and not something to be talked about openly and freely. As these baby boomers entered into a season of life where they found spiritual interests to be a much more significant component of their identity, they found faith storytelling to be an inevitable next step.

Jean shared that she learned from her dad that faith is private, where "you don't impose it on other people," including in your own home. This led Jean to always keep her faith "very private." Yet, as Jean has grown in her spiritual interests along with concern for the eternal future of her grandchildren, she sees a change in her value chain. Jean says that she is "concerned" about her grandchildren, especially "those that that don't know the Lord." Jean is willing to make her faith public so her grandchildren are introduced to her Christian faith.

Jean looks back on the time when her children were growing up in her home as a lost opportunity to live out her faith in a way that her children could more readily observe. They attended church, but she did not experience or express robust faith in the home. Jean now sees her faith as a key part of her identity which she is increasingly looking to express in public—even though it goes against her childhood socialization.

The interesting connection for Jean with community service and mission opportunities is that she engaged in both of those during mid-life adulthood. She continues to see the benefit of that engagement in terms of service provided and also an ability for her to use her skills for good. Yet, she looks back with regret that her priorities were on doing good things rather than living out a faith-filled identity. She sees her current volunteering as much different than earlier in life. Jean is now focused on serving God and living out who she thinks God has called her to be, rather than doing good things to earn some religious credits. Similar to her interest in sharing faith with her grandchildren, Jean's identity as a Christian has grown to where she wants to publicly communicate her faith through service.

The change in identity that leads to faith storytelling was significant among participants. Twenty-eight participants mentioned the growing importance of being able to share their story with individuals who are relationally close to them. Their identity as a Christian is so central and significant now that they want to make sure that their family is well aware of what their faith means. Joe has become so passionate about this core identity as a Christian that he created a video for his children and grandchildren where he tells his life story along with changes in his faith over his life span. Although he is disappointed with the limited conversations that have been sparked with family members, he is pleased that he has been transparent about his Christian identity.

Sixteen participants shared stories about how they have increased in their public faith storytelling. Similar to Jean, many baby boomers have linked their public service to public faith sharing. All told, we see that the vast majority of participants (twenty-seven of the thirty-one) saw their public practice of faith through service opportunities changed by an identity shift, while over half (sixteen of thirty-one) observed that their public proclamation of faith significantly changed. An interesting twist with storytelling is that many baby boomers in this study observed how much they learned about their change in identity through the storytelling process. After interviews, I received a number of cards and emails thanking me for providing a safe place for them to tell their story—and to gain a better understanding of their religious identity and how it has changed over recent years.

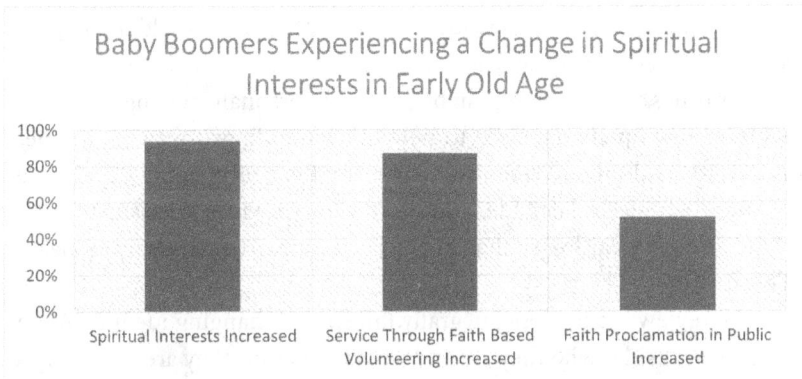

**Baby Boomers Experiencing a Change in Spiritual Interests in Early Old Age**

## Life Review and Personal Legacy

The rise of prominence and centrality of religious identity that comes with aging has been established. We now turn to the increase in the practice of life review that takes place with aging. I want to pause here for a bit and delve into what exactly is meant by the term "life review" as it has significance for better connecting with adults about their spiritual life. Hopefully the methodology that I used in the research is a helpful framework to use in other rural settings as we engage with adults.

Life review is a gerontological narrative approach[5] where an older person is guided in telling their own story, including their self-evaluation and meaning making of that story.[6] Life review is anchored to original contributions by Robert Butler. Similar to developmental psychologists, Butler maintains that there is "the universal occurrence in older people of an inner experience or mental process of reviewing one's life."[7] Life review is seen as an inevitable part of the aging process where "the biological fact of approaching death, independent of—although possibly reinforced by—personal and environmental circumstances prompts the life review."[8]

Life review is not necessarily a clean snapshot, nor replaying of the movie film from one's life. It involves stray thoughts that come back to one's mind—sometimes seemingly insignificant things. Since life review entails reconsideration of life events and attempting to make sense of the meaning behind experiences[9] I needed to patiently listen and encourage storytelling rather than a chronological listing of events. Sometimes this sense-making can involve recreating the past into the good old days, where history is treated as malleable and shaped into what the person wants it to be; other times sense-making can be a time of personality change, in which the life review opens the door to new understandings—moving the person toward wisdom and serenity.[10] There are long-term aging experiences that shape people in later life, and life review provides a means to move beyond the physical losses that might be recounted exclusively to hear a fuller story.[11]

Life review is a process integrally linked to a changing identity. As aging people consider who they are and what they value, they are also likely to look back over their lives to seek to establish the value of their lives. Indeed,

5. Ramsey and Bliezner, *Spiritual Resiliency and Aging*, 38; Weil, *Research Design in Aging*, 51; Butler, "Life Review," 65–76.

6. Weil, *Research Design in Aging*, 51.

7. Butler, "Life Review," 65.

8. Butler, "Life Review," 67.

9. Butler, "Life Review," 68.

10. Butler, "Life Review," 69, 75.

11. Butler, "Life Review," 75.

twenty-eight of the thirty-one participants shared stories that reflected a life review—sense making of the life journey that they had been on up to this point and the reason that they are still alive.

Rick provides a great example of the life review interest that comes with aging. He now finds himself asking the question "why am I still here?" This is a question that he "never thought too much about it until more recent, as in the last two years." At this point in life, he cannot shake this question because, as he states, it's what happens as "ya get a little bit older and git thinkin about where ya been and what you did."

The vast majority of baby boomers in this study mentioned that they were much more reflective of their past, yearning to observe how they ended up where they are today and what their purpose in life is for their final years. A linked theme that emerged with this life review was one of personal legacy. Many baby boomers talked about how pausing and reflecting about the meaning of their lives led them to identify a number of areas in their lives in which their values were misplaced. Time and again, these misplaced values circled around a desire to establish a personal legacy that was more timeless.

Harold shared his story of misplaced values. From the vantage point of career goals, he far surpassed his early life expectations. Harold worked in finance and was able to navigate up the corporate chain to a position of senior leadership in a large company. Looking back though, Harold has found that his "ladder" was resting on the wrong building. He worked hard to climb the ladder of corporate success, and despite that success, found that it came at a cost to his family and faith life. Now that he has retired to part-time consulting work, Harold regrets the long days, taking work with him on vacations, and the total consumption of his thought life that his work demanded. As he works through life review, he realizes that the personal legacy he wants to leave is through his family and memories of his faithful living. Realizing that he cannot go back to right previous wrongs, Harold now sees an identity shift as he focuses on spiritual matters like never before in his life, including public witness of his faith.

The matter of the ladder was shared by those in more traditional rural occupations as well. One farmer, Rob, spoke of how much of his farming career was designed to build an empire. He loves farming and put in long hours and networked aggressively to be able to build his acreage and compete in the agribusiness world as economies of scale became increasingly important. As the years went by and life review increased, Rob began to realize that he was chasing the wrong dream. His love for farming has not changed, but the value he places on it has changed.

At the time of the interview Rob talked about his current retirement process in which he is liquidating his farm assets and retiring. The farming legacy of his family is ending, but he has lowered the value of that in shaping his overall identity. In fact, Rob talked a great deal about wanting his legacy to be more than farming. He is considering volunteering with Hospice and other opportunities to provide faith support to others as his own faith continues to grow. Rob's identity has shifted as the value he places on relationships increased, and the legacy that he wants to leave is less tethered to farming. This is especially evident when it comes to his children.

## Children, Grandchildren, and Security

Rob was glowing about his son and daughter. He shared multiple positive stories about the faith of his children and how proud he is of them. In particular, he talked at length about the joy he has as he continues to watch his children grow in their faith. One particular joy for Rob during the interview was that his son would be leading a campus ministry for the first time that very night. While that received a lot of emphasis in our conversation, Rob mentioned, in a matter-of-fact manner, that his son had returned from college as an employee on the farm, would not be taking over the farm, and that he would seek other employment as the farm was sold. There was not a desire to cover up this cause of the farm legacy ending, and yet, it was not an emotional concern—at least the way that Rob told the story. It seems as though Rob's identity is focused on more spiritual matters than the farming legacy that once drove him from pre-dawn to post-dusk.

Rob's connection between change in personal legacy and concern for children or grandchildren was shared by many—twenty-seven of the thirty-one baby boomers shared stories about the change in their concern for next generations of their family. Two of the women who were not included in the twenty-seven did not have children, but have deeply invested themselves in relationships with children through local schools.

The concern for children and grandchildren is different than caregiving—concern focuses more on a desire to bless one's family through sharing faith or strengthening faith rather than meeting a physical need. We have already seen concern for the next generation through the story of Jean wanting to share her faith with her grandchildren or Harold wanting to live out his faith for his adult children to observe change in his life.

This is not to indicate that these baby boomers were necessarily disengaged from their families. Becky talks about how she was completely engaged in her children's lives when they were growing up—if they were involved in something, she was a parent volunteer. Becky punctuates her level of volunteering by saying "that was my life when my kids were growing up." Yet, this investment was more to shape good kids, not necessarily to form faith. This group of baby boomers indicated that they now consider a part of their legacy as leaving faith with their children and grandchildren. They want to convey their stories in ways that prevent next generations from wandering as long as they did without a well-developed faith. The role of concern about next generations highlights the potential importance of youth ministry—just not for where we usually put the sole emphasis. The grandparents are a spiritual sensitive group that are likely candidates to invite as participants.

## Summary of Identity

Stories of identity shift were a prevalent theme associated with aging in this study. The recurrence of this theme indicates that life review is a very real process that shapes the value chain. Baby boomers are not likely to reference a significant addition of religious values. The change takes place through valuing elements of their religious identity more and reducing the value of some of the criteria that they used for measuring success during much of their adult lives—from career milestones to family achievements.

As baby boomers increasingly value their religious identity, they feel that they are increasingly overt in sharing their faith. The role of identity was observed in pastor interviews as well. Some mentioned the transition into early old age as similar to the transition from middle school to high school—there is a change of peer relationships, expectations, and physical changes that bring about a reflection on who you are and the image you want to project.

# CHAPTER 6

# Silver Mission Characteristics

L ET'S examine our rural ministry toolbox. We have established that we often hold on to stereotypical rural ministry tools regardless of community demographics at the cost of missing missional opportunities. The missed rural ministry opportunity for the rural church is Silver Mission: *adults transitioning into early old age are sensitive to the gospel message like no other time since the four to fourteen age-window.*

I am similar to many church leaders: I have listened to hours of podcasts and panel discussions and consumed countless books about how our churches need to be more relevant in the community today. Usually that discussion focuses on how the congregation has "grayed" and is drawing few young families, so we should be ashamed. There is truth in the need to reach kids between the ages of four and fourteen with the gospel —but it should not come at the expense of intentionally drawing adults who are nearing or recently entered retirement. There may actually be equivalent shame in *not* reaching older adults.

The following are five characteristics of missional churches that are successfully drawing retirement age adults into their congregations. These churches are reaching non-Christian or nominally Christian adults who subsequently come to a vibrant Christian faith in later adulthood.

1. Recognize "early old age" as a demographic. Early old age is a new cultural phenomena: the postretirement time period stretching from age sixty-five to eighty where there are a number of life changes that take place bringing freedom, yet precedes a number of "care-dependency

needs" that rise more dramatically after age eighty.[1] This is a new span of life in American history, but the church is missing it. The specific study of ministry with this young-old time period has been minimal and has generated little documentation.[2]

Not only is there little study of ministry and early old age, but there is also a general lack of emphasis by churches. For instance, ask yourself a question. Does my church provide ministry opportunity specifically for the early old age? Generally, churches are very good at providing ministry *to* adults who need assistance that comes with age related changes. Churches have not been so quick to provide ministry *with* the early old age group. The church generally tries to minister *to* anyone in older age, including the early old age category. Early old age individuals have life experiences, talents, and skills that can bless the church during a unique season of retirement or semi-retirement, yet the church only offers ministry to opportunities.

If your church provides these ministry opportunities, you are in a select group of churches! What I am getting at here is intentionality with early old age. If it is not intentional, we tend to provide services to this group. We assume that younger people are the ones that we intentionally reach out to, and that we have older people figured out because that's who tends to be in our churches. But are we mobilizing this age group to its potential? Likewise, are we reaching this age group who is part of the "done's" — people who left the church earlier in life due to dissatisfaction but are now reconsidering their faith?

2. Provide a place to belong. The primary focus of churches on a silver mission is to provide a place to *belong*. Most early old age adults now coming to faith have left church at some point across their youth or adult years. They need a compelling reason to return—but promoting Christian beliefs and Christian behavior are insufficient on their own.

---

1. Dillon and Wink, *In the Course of a Lifetime*, 137.
2. Dillon and Wink, *In the Course of a Lifetime*, 137.

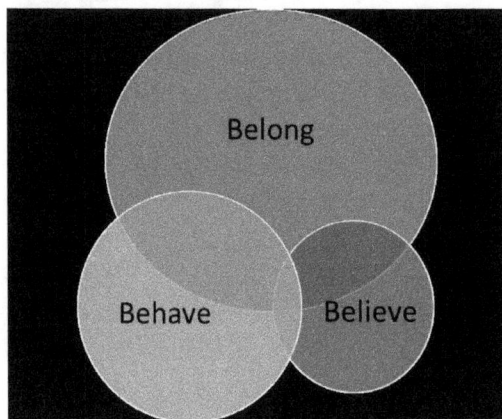

**Venn Diagram of Religiosity**

Make no mistake, silver mission churches encourage change in *behavior* that range from moral lifestyle choices to increasing spiritual practices such as prayer. Silver mission churches also are clear and up front about orthodox *beliefs*. These tenets of behavior and belief are not entirely new to these adults who have largely grown up within the church—though their understanding of the gospel is often truncated as good works and moralism.

What early old age adults highlight as the most important pull factor to a church is the authentic experience of community that highlights the application of behavior and beliefs. There is not a certain sequence of belonging, believing, and behaving that draws adults to church—these components of faith are all at work simultaneously. The focus on belonging is what makes the difference among silver mission churches, and the approach to belonging is very specific.

3. Focus on loss, not gain. That is right—losses are more important than gains. Let me explain. As people age, they are naturally going to try to maximize their gains in life, such as extra time in retirement, connecting with grandchildren, or savoring the afterglow of a great career.[3] At the same time, they are going to compensate for losses that take place: death of loved ones, decline of personal health, loss of relationships at retirement, along with hushed losses such as sex drive.

---

3. For more information on this concept of "Selective Optimization with Compensation" see: Baltes et al., "Life Span Theory in Developmental Psychology," 569–659.

Here is the deal when it comes to belonging to a church: we do not compete well when it comes to gains. A summer home on the lake near grandchildren versus a Bible Study is not naturally going to yield to increased belonging at church. Losses are much more likely to yield belonging—but only with intentionality.

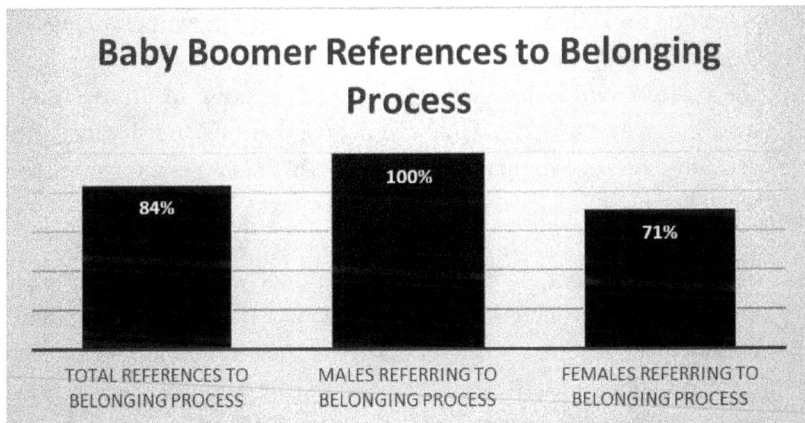

Baby Boomer References to Belonging Process

The two most significant losses that lead to belonging are: death of a loved one and decline in personal health. The death of a loved one leads to a hunger for belonging to a faith-based support group. Personal decline in health creates a desire to engage in a small group that practices and models prayer. It is during seasons of loss that there is spiritual sensitivity—an individual grapples with deep relational loss, is wondering why life is happening a certain way, and also begins to consider their own mortality. Finally, the individual is not going to instantly join a church—but they are very likely to join a small group if they are invited while dealing with loss.

4. Informal small groups that offer a safe place and "challenge not chaplaincy."[4] Rural churches effectively engaged in the silver mission recognize that many people entering early old age have been burned by a church in their past—at least from their own perspective. On top of that, many people in this age bracket are wary of any organizational

4. Mills et al., "Listening and Enabling," 54.

structure after living through the 1960s, the Watergate era, and their own corporate experience.

The most welcoming small groups are clearly faith based, but not an explicit ministry of the church. This is not a bait and switch approach—the Christian foundation is explicit. There is an informal feel through no business meetings, no officers, no committees, and very little organizational structure that is discussed with participants. While the informal nature of the group matters, it is also critical that the place is safe. With many participants looking to process their losses, they want to know that the people that they are sharing with are authentic and mutually vulnerable. There is a need for ministry *with*, and not ministry *to* through this context.

A corollary to informal is "challenge not chaplaincy." Not only are individuals looking to work through their wounds, but they also want to make a difference. Early old age is a new cultural phenomenon—there are many years of active life post-retirement or during semi-retirement where people yearn to impact the lives of others. The small group design needs to bridge beyond a self-help group and offer opportunities to make a difference in other people's lives.

If the only focus is on getting people to belong with other people facing similar losses, the engagement ends up being short-term or the individual remains at a surface level of belonging. The pathway to deeper belonging is through service projects. When there is an opportunity to help with a broader endeavor, such as a community-oriented project, there is a challenge to engage in that provides purpose and meaning, even amidst loss.

Not only that, but service projects are great equalizers and bridgers. Whether someone is a long-term church goer or a small group attendee, they are on equal footing when it comes to sweating through a short-term project. This also provides the small group attendee an opportunity to "try out" using their skills, talents, and abilities for a greater purpose. When someone feels like they are no longer just a recipient of chaplaincy, their sense of belonging increases with the challenge. Likewise, the equal footing in the project offers a bridger opportunity where people can get to know one another in a casual setting, which is a useful counter to being labeled as or feeling like an outsider.

Silver mission churches provide an intentional pathway for early old age individuals to belong. There are small groups for people to process their losses. There are mid-sized service groups where people engage in a short-term project with people they do not know as well. The weekly worship service provides a hub of unique community that people engage in more deeply and consistently as the small groups and service groups open doors to broadened relationships. The importance of a belonging process is especially strong among men.

5. Faith commitment is presented as a life-course journey over a decision-event. The vast majority of early old age adults were brought up attending church at least sporadically. Most grew up and retained identification as a Christian—even if they were not practicing that faith most of their lives. Rural churches that are seeing the most success welcoming mature adults into belonging take individuals' stories seriously, including their backstory.

Rather than acting as though someone in their sixties has never heard a Bible story or has never had some sort of faith experience, effective churches invite people to tell their story. Some of the most innovative approaches to blending small groups and deepening faith commitment involve storytelling. Even before someone has publicly professed faith in Jesus Christ as Lord and Savior, these churches are providing opportunities for people to tell their faith story. Where do they sense God leading them on their journey? Where have they witnessed God's hand in their lives? It is through processing their own story in community that many have come to recognize their desire for an authentic relationship with Jesus Christ.

The storytelling does not stop there. The silver mission churches continue encouraging individuals to share their story post-conversion. A key is through training or providing technological tools to help individuals record their story digitally. In turn, these early old age individuals who are experiencing a new sense of belonging share their life journey with family and friends and express why their lives are different now. One of the most often mentioned goals for early old age individuals is that their grandchildren will hear their story.

## PRACTICAL

Think about this in terms of billboards. What matters with a billboard is how many visual impressions it generates. The size, location, road traffic, etc. are important factors, but what ultimately matters is the metric involving visual impressions—how many people actually take it in. The same is similar for baby-boomers and reengaging faith. Just because baby-boomers have been around churches for a long time does not mean that they have actually taken in visual impressions. Even more importantly, it is possible that the only visual impressions of Christianity have been a counterfeit, and not based on gospel truth.

We need to take a hard look at this concept of cultural Christian heartlands in the light that Leslie Newbigin sheds on it. There is a need "to recognize that the most urgent contemporary mission field is to be found in their own traditional heartlands, and that the most aggressive paganism with which they have to engage is the ideology that now controls the 'developed' world."[5] Rather than simply writing off the people who have only attended services at Christmas and Easter for decades in our "heartland" communities, we need to take this window of spiritual sensitivity to reintroduce people to Jesus.

The following chart provides opportunities based on the data presented where churches can be intentional to provide targeted visual impressions for adults as they journey in life. The "shaping influence" column contains life events (or series of events) that push toward spiritual sensitivity. The "belonging opportunities" column contains pull factors that churches can offer to specifically reach out to people who are spiritually sensitive and in turn sensitive to finding a place to belong. The column entitled "most spiritually sensitive to influence" contains the subset of the population who are most likely to be pushed toward faith by the specific shaping influences. Finally, the "specific interests" column highlights effective pull factors that churches can offer to people who are being pushed toward spiritual conversations and possibly belonging to a faith community.

5. Newbigin, *Gospel in a Pluralist Society*, 10.

| Shaping Influence | Belonging Opportunities | Most Spiritually Sensitive to Influence | Specific Interests |
|---|---|---|---|
| Death | Small Group | Socially distanced from church | Short-term desire for spiritual support |
| Illness of others | Prayer Group | Most rural areas | Increasing emotional support from church |
| Personal Health | Intimate Power Encounters | Most rural areas | Heightened desire to change lifestyle |
| Caregiving | Small Group | Least rural areas | Grandchild focused in least rural, parent focused in most rural |
| Divorce | Small Group | Self-identified | Heightened desire to change lifestyle |
| Spiritual Identity Change | Service Groups | Early old age | Purpose through missional work |

**Church Ministry Opportunities**

# SECTION 2

SECTION 2

# CHAPTER 7

# Communication

O NE more question is worthwhile to consider as we start thinking about communication. This wildfire story pointed out the tragic focus on the task of fire control while responsibility to crew and safety was a distant second. As rural pastors and congregants caught in the wildfire of these times, how can our priorities reflect a similar focus?

## PRACTICE COMMUNICATION

Realizing that the crew would not make it to safety, Dodge stopped, took out matches, and did what few people had ever done before. He started another fire. He lit wild grass on fire to create an escape fire. He beckoned the others to join him in this space where the fuel for the wildfire was now gone, but they thought that he was crazy to start another fire and jump in behind it. As Dodge wet the handkerchief over his face and lay down as close to the ground and remaining oxygen as he could, the rest of the Smokejumpers sought to outrun the blaze.[1] The lack of two key communication foundations fed into these choices: just cause and trust.

*Just cause.* The Smokejumpers had been coached on the usefulness of the tools and the financial cost of the tools, not trained on times where the tools could be a detriment. This training is reinforced by social pressure if the people ahead of them continue to carry their tools rather than setting them down. Alongside this is the sense that dropping tools seems like an

---

1. Turner, "Thirteenth Fire," 27. Grant, *Think Again*, 2.

insignificant change that is unlikely to provide significant benefits. We will stick with an overlearned behavior rather than do something new.[2]

Dodge did not keep the crew briefed during the incident. Without a "why" behind the commands of drop the tools and lie down in the escape fire, they did not make sense.[3] Dodge felt that the dangers were so obvious that a reason for dropping tools was not needed. Yet, nine of the fifteen were first year jumpers, and all of them were trained for timber firefighting, not the grassland that they were now in.[4]

What Dodge intuitively saw, but the rest of the crew missed, was a change of context.[5] If anything, the crew should have been more attuned to their context since the Smoke Jumpers had not even been provided with maps during the rushed preparation for the jump.[6] The crew was also isolated from the outside world since the parachute for the radio had failed to open.[7]

With all of these communication items working against them, why would they not be ready to listen well? The Smokejumper's reputation as fire experts prevented them from seeing what they did not know about a wildfire "blowup" that was taking place.[8] Science surrounding wildfire blowups was not understood until the 1950s but the Smokejumpers did not have a posture of listening.[9] Because of limited scientific study, no one grasped that the wind conditions had created a "blow-up" where the fire was rapidly expanding—the 1,500 to 1,800 degree Fahrenheit fire was covering about three thousand acres in ten minutes.[10] While Dodge did not understand the mechanics of a blowup, he did recognize the dangers of the context. No longer were they protected from the wind by trees, they were now in fast burning cheat grass, and not within the boundaries of a forest fire that they had been trained for.[11]

---

2. Weick, "Drop Your Tools," 306–7.

3. Weick, "Drop Your Tools," 305.

4. Weick, "Drop Your Tools," 305–6.

5. Maclean, *Young Men and Fire*, 40.

6. Maclean, *Young Men and Fire*, 43.

7. Maclean, *Young Men and Fire*, 56.

8. Maclean, *Young Men and Fire*, 19, 33.

9. Maclean, *Young Men and Fire*, 87.

10. Lehman, "August 5, 1949."

11. Schulz, "Story That Tore Through the Trees"; Maclean, *Young Men and Fire*.

Dodge had the posture of learning and a lens of experience to observe the danger—a posture and lens that the rest of the crew were not utilizing. Dodge missed that he needed to be preparing his crew for this moment by communicating the obvious before they reached a time in which the noise of the close fire would prevent meaningful communication between people.[12] The roar of the fire, the rush of the wind, and the frantic panting of men on the run created a noise that drowned out Dodge's pleas.

*Trust.* "People persist when they don't trust the person that tells them to change." There was not trust between Dodge and the crew because of limited training time together.[13] On the one hand, Dodge did not communicate with providing just cause, but he was not placed in a position to do so with ample time. The limited training time together was exacerbated by no training aimed to build a sense of team nor upon how to take orders.[14]

Since trust was not built, Dodge stood up all alone from his experimental escape fire patch fifteen minutes after he called out to others to join him. Through the tragic turn of events, thirteen others would perish.[15] Wagner Dodge's example was not followed. Even his words went unheeded. If the crew had listened rather than thinking he was crazy, they could have survived.[16] Just cause was not communicated to the crew, and that was enhanced by a lack of trust.

As rural ministry practitioners, we have some important questions to ask in regard to communication. How healthy is my communication? Do I provide just cause for why we do what we do in ministry? Am I investing in relationships in a way that builds trust and is not simply aimed at task completion? Finally, what are unique ministry opportunities that God is inviting you and I to communicate in this season? We need to be honest about the noise around us and the change of context. Intentionality behind our communication is necessary—and our experience over the last few years should push us ever further into that space.

---

12. Maclean, *Young Men and Fire*, 72.

13. Weick, "Drop Your Tools," 306; Maclean, *Young Men and Fire*, 40.

14. Maclean, *Young Men and Fire*, 101, 219.

15. Grant, *Think Again*, 2.

16. Maclean, *Young Men and Fire*, 96, 99, 100; Grant, *Think Again*,.

# CHAPTER 8

# Communicating Just Cause

M ANY rural ministry books are effective and helpful in looking at practical tools we can use to have gospel impact in our communities. What we are aiming to do in this book is to actually step back and examine the toolbox itself—not just the application of our tools. As introduced in the story of the Mann Gulch fire, we are not inclined to drop our tools, or for that matter, pick up tools that are more effective for this season. There are some essential tools that we oftentimes skip over when talking about rural ministry. How do we assess faith among rural residents? Is it only what they claim to believe through surveys? Or is faith best measured by how often someone attends a worship service? Answering these questions are critical to understand our tools and communicate faith authentically in rural communities. It is from this foundation that we are able to communicate with just cause.

## DEFINING FAITH: BELONGING, BELIEVING, AND BEHAVING

This brings us to defining what we are assessing in regard to the Christian faith. *Religiosity* is the objective term commonly measured in research, using the framework of belonging, believing, and behaving.[1] We will examine each of these manifestations of faith, and begin opening the door to making sure we are aware of the tools in our box.

1. Olson and Warber, "Belonging, Behaving, and Believing"; Putnam and Campbell, *American Grace*; Seversen, "Millennials Connecting to Contemporary Congregations," 224.

## BELONGING

Joseph Myers defines belonging as what "happens when you identify with another entity—a person or organization, or perhaps a species, culture, or ethnic group."[2] When it comes to religiosity, belonging is a key element assessed to establish the saliency of faith identification by the individual and the centrality of their Christian social integration. Hence, belonging is measured by variables such as church attendance.[3]

Let's not pass over this step too quickly though—there is nuance to defining what "church attendance" constitutes. Attendance can include: the large group weekly worship service, the moderately sized service groups, the small groups where there is in-depth study and conversation with other people, as well as very intimate groups who gather to talk with authenticity and vulnerability.[4] We will take a look at each of these places to belong, and how they are unique tools in the box.

### Worship Services

The nature of worship services can seem so obvious that we overlook the unique opportunity for belonging that they offer. The large worship service offers "scale anonymity." People can safely come to "try out church" through engagement at their own pace. Without the social pressures of smaller contexts, people are able to engage at a level in which personalized responses are not pressed upon them.[5] Although a potentially low-cost investment, worship service attendance is a key cultural marker of where one "belongs."

### Service Groups

Belonging to moderately-sized service group serves as a marker for many people returning to church later in life, or even post-COVID. People are

2. Myers, *Search to Belong*, 25.

3. Seversen, "Millennials Connecting to Contemporary Congregations," 224; Bengtson et al., "Does Religiousness Increase with Age?," 367; Hayward and Krause, "Aging, Social Developmental, and Cultural Factors," 984.

4. Myers, *Search to Belong*; McNeal, "Missional Communities—European Style"; Myers, *Organic Community*; Harrington and Absalom, *Discipleship That Fits*; For more information about the influence of proxemics see Hall, *Hidden Dimension*, 123–25, 121–23, 119–20, 116–19; Myers, *Search to Belong*, 20; Hall, "Proxemics."

5. Harrington and Absalom, *Discipleship That Fits*, 76.

increasingly cause-oriented rather than program-motivated. There is a desire for meaningful activity that is relationship based, leading to a desire to belong to a group rather than join an organization. Adults often desire to shape the activities they participate in and not have them dictated to them by an authority.[6] Many rural residents find a home in a mission-oriented group that is based on a network of relationships, is lightweight and low-maintenance in organizational structure, and feels more like a lifestyle than a program.[7]

Belonging is facilitated when the emphasis is on mission *with* adults, not *to* the 'lowly people' who are outside the church.[8] In rural ministry where many locations are witnessing a rise in average age and number of retirees, this is a key aspect to pay attention to. Given the changes in life-expectancy and characteristics of baby boomers, it is important to target early retirement baby boomers as participants rather than recipients.[9] Youth ministry and baby boomers offer an interesting missional intersection for baby boomers to belong and grow; Ammerman states:

> Most congregations think of 'young families' as a sign of their vitality, and this is so—not because those families represent a guarantee for future survival, but because the impulse to provide one's children with religious education is one of the primary incentives for adult religious participation.[10]

Service opportunities for adults to work with youth is not only for the benefit of their grandchildren. Youth-oriented service offers opportunities for the adults themselves to sense an increased sense of belonging. This is not to belittle youth ministry—but to recognize it is not the only tool at our disposal. We do rural churches a disservice if we neglect the number of older adults who are distanced from church and are looking for an entry point to belong to a faith community.

6. McIntosh, "Trends and Challenges for Ministry," 297.

7. Breen, *Leading Missional Communities*, 8–10.

8. McIntosh, "Trends and Challenges for Ministry," 297.

9. Vanderstelt, *Saturate*, 220–24.

10. Ammerman, *Congregation & Community*, 58.

## Small Groups

Rural residents are likely to belong to small groups when they have a need of people to be "in person" in their lives, especially as friends and family move away, or die. The capacity to develop new supportive friendships is increasingly critical as people age.[11] In a British study, "Bereavement was found to be a key time for the questioning of faith and belief, and the researchers were surprised to discover how little contact had been made with participants by religious leaders."[12] Hence, the role of small groups intersects rising losses of aging and the practice of compensating for those losses through deeper, more vulnerable relationships.[13]

## Intimate Groups

People are lonely. That is true across communities and is especially true in our rural communities. Let's take a look at the elderly once again, but this time people who are part of a church and still find themselves alone. In an English study of sixty lay church members aged sixty and older, 90 percent said that they were lonely or marginalized at times within their own church. The top remedies to this feeling of marginalization were through the intimate context where individual contact was maintained through visitation and befriending.[14] The importance of tight-knit connection goes beyond church members. There are also community members who self-identify as belonging to a church because a member of the church has befriended them and walked with them through difficult times—even if they have never met most of the individual members of the congregation.[15] Myers offers a rural anecdote to frame today's nostalgic appeal of belonging:

> Being alone. This was something that never concerned most farmers of the past. The family stayed home. As life progressed, no one ever thought about being alone. The kids were given plots 'on the back forty' to build a home and raise a family. When mom and dad could no longer work, the boys took over and cared for the

11. Edward, "Friends in Old Age," 198.

12. Rolph et al., "What Churches May Have," 61, 70.

13. Baltes et al., "Life Span Theory in Developmental Psychology"; English and Carstensen, "Selective Narrowing of Social Networks."

14. Rolph et al., "What Churches May Have," 69–70.

15. Myers, *Search to Belong*, 29.

land and the old folks as well. Not so today. And this cultural shift is a major factor in our struggle to belong. People are trying to find their place in this world, not in individualist ways but in ways that connect. They are searching for the 'back forty,' for a place to belong. They are searching for family.[16]

We will continue to come back to the theme of belonging. All too often we run past the multiple layers of belonging to a church. We can become so focused on one type of belonging that we do not drop that tool at the right time. We can become so fixated on the number of people who gather for weekly worship that we miss the need for lonely people to be in small groups. On the other hand, we can become so oriented to the relational needs met through intimate groups that we neglect other avenues of belonging. Likewise, we can also miss the "less churchy" opportunities for adults to belong to more informally organized service groups.

## BELIEVING

Believing is measured by cognitive aspects such as self-identified beliefs, self-identified intensity of belief,[17] as well as assessments of adherence to traditional, orthodox Christian beliefs.[18] For many rural residents, Jesus is not totally unknown. We need to be sure that when we talk about someone "believing" that we take a look at their life story and trajectory of beliefs, not simply what they say on a given day.

The baby boomer generation is a large portion of many of our rural communities and is worth using as an example. Nearly 95 percent of the baby boomer generation was raised in homes with religious affiliation;[19] even more, some studies state that two-thirds of baby boomer respondents (67 percent) indicate that their childhood experience included religious service attendance at a frequency of at least often or very often.[20] But this does not equate orthodox belief.

16. Myers, *Search to Belong*, 26.

17. Silverstein and Bengtson, "Return to Religion?," 11; Bengtson et al., "Does Religiousness Increase with Age?," 367; Hayward and Krause, "Aging, Social Developmental, and Cultural Factors," 984.

18. Smith and Snell, *Souls in Transition*, 124, 135.

19. Schwadel, "Age, Period, and Cohort Effects," 314. Putnam and Campbell, 147–48.

20. Silverstein and Bengtson, "Return to Religion?," 15.

Whether a baby boomer or from another generation cohort, previous religious socialization presents the hazard of "inoculation" where religiously socialized persons view Christianity as something which is known and previously rejected.[21] Perceptions linger from childhood encounters that may have been more cultural than truly experiential, resulting in a false perception of biblical Christian faith. Hence, many rural residents have a mixed bag of biblical literacy and familiarity with Christian faith that needs to be taken into account as they talk about faith.

Self-identified Christian beliefs can be incredibly variant and unorthodox even though orthodox terminology or Bible passages are used. Many may identify as having continued believing, but the "character of their belief" changed.[22] Individualism and personal freedom have encouraged a shift away from religious orthodoxy and proscribed faith, from beliefs as objective truth to feelings. What is right for me becomes a primary assessment.[23] Taken a step further, there are more options and social acceptance to pursue a variety of religious beliefs and practices, in which one can pick and choose from the buffet table of religious beliefs.[24] In the end, the blend of individualism and pluralism has developed into a focus on personal experience over following orthodox church doctrine and teaching.[25] Someone who self-ascribes as a Christian may actually adhere to a pragmatic approach to religion[26] rather than an orthodox statement of faith. In rural ministry, we must listen closely for what "belief" means rather than taking glow words from the Bible at face value.

## BEHAVING

Behaving is measured by variables such as level of volunteering[27] and actions. Behaving through volunteering and life actions allow nonbelievers

---

21. Gustafson, *Gospel Witness*, 5. See also Hollinghurst, *Mission-Shaped Evangelism*, 190.

22. Hunter, "What is Modernity?" 25.

23. Smith and Snell, *Souls in Transition*, 156.

24. Newbigin, *Gospel in a Pluralist Society*, 168; Smith and Snell, *Souls in Transition*, 144–48.

25. Bengtson et al., "Does Religiousness Increase with Age?," 366. Smith and Snell, *Souls in Transition*, 290–91.

26. Bengtson et al., "Does Religiousness Increase with Age?," 376.

27. Silverstein and Bengtson, "Return to Religion?," 12.

to be able "try out a Christian identity before committing to it."[28] Behaving can also be assessed through questions that identify components of the moral lifestyle of participants.[29]

An assessment of behaving leads us to look through the lens of "everyday religion." The focus is on the lived experience of nonexperts in the world of religious ideas, but are simultaneously experts about their own story.[30] The focus is on individual life stories while also listening for how a person's context shapes their everyday life.[31] "Practicing religion focuses on what people do and say rather than only on what they think and believe."[32] The "practice turn" advocated by Ammerman and Wuthnow emphasizes the old adage: "Your walk walks, and your talk talks, but does your walk talk?" Behaving provides indicators of the authenticity of believing and belonging.

In addition to moral lifestyle, volunteering, and life actions, behavior is reflected through the practice of rituals—and intersects with both believing and belonging. For instance, rituals substantively connect people with the sacred, and are practices to guide people into a sense of belonging to God. There is also a significant functional role of rituals which impacts the sense of belonging to a group. Whether it is the Lord's Prayer, recitation of creeds, the Lord's Supper, standing for hymns, or reading Scripture, there are traditional practices that shape one's faith. Ritual provides remembering a group's heritage and commonly held convictions. There is social bonding that takes place through performing these practices together in community and as one body. There is also an element of socialization linked with change in status, such as through baptism or marriage.[33]

Stick with me here—I realize that ritual is a bad word for many of us looking to shake hollow cultural traditions in our context. However, tradition and ritual does not need to equate to hollow and meaningless. The practice of rituals can have significance to the religiously socialized rural residents.

28. Seversen, "Millennials Connecting to Contemporary Congregations," 231, 234.

29. Smith and Snell, *Souls in Transition*, 265–75.

30. Ammerman, "Observing Religious Modern Lives," 5.

31. Ammerman, "Observing Religious Modern Lives," 6; Wuthnow, *What Happens When We Practice*, 2–4. Ammerman, "Rethinking Religion."

32. Wuthnow, *What Happens When We Practice*, 1.

33. Swenson, *Society, Spirituality, and the Sacred*, 186; Swart, "Social Capital," 241–43; Cilliers and Wepener, "Ritual and the Generation."

"Word and ritual go together. The word communicates to the verbal and cognitive side of the person, whereas the symbol or ritual communicates to the emotive side of the person. The issue is not either/or but both/and."[34] Attention to both the cognitive and practical pushes us back to the importance of qualitative research. As sociologist Robert Wuthnow states, "Qualitative studies bring possibilities of closer attention to *how* people talk about and enact religious practices and how those practices intersect with ordinary life."[35]

We are not just dealing with semantics here. Rural ministry practitioners can quickly run to the latest survey of self-described beliefs in rural America as the description of faith trends in their own community. Or we can use our handy laptop to access lots of data about church attendance in rural America, thinking that the percentage of those attending gathered worship services is the primary definition of opportunities and challenges to ministry in our community. When we add in assessing behavior as part of assessing faith in rural communities, we see the complexity and start to see more opportunities to reach for some different ministry tools. Examining behavior as a part of rural ministry assessment leads us to realize that we are not just assessing a geographic location, but also the people. We need to listen to the stories of individuals and the story of a community to better grasp how God is at work in and through the people of this place.

Part of the complexity that we need to face involves investigating a counter-intuitive opportunity. When rural residents say that they are spiritual but not religious, we can take that as completely disinterested in the church, and a daunting challenge that is only increasing. When we take belonging, believing, and behaving into account, we actually see the opportunity that is on the rise for rural ministry.

One of the key areas that we need to grapple with in this season is the rising phenomenon of "spiritual but not religious." More and more Americans are labeling themselves as spiritual but want to have nothing to do with the church. This is true in rural America—and is actually a tremendous opportunity for us to consider, if we are willing to communicate differently.

34. Webber, *Ancient-Future Evangelism*, 49.
35. Wuthnow, *What Happens When We Practice*, 195.

# CHAPTER 9

# Communicating Trust

## SPIRITUAL BUT NOT RELIGIOUS?

R URAL churches have a window of opportunity to invite people to belong—the sweet spot of the overlap between spiritual *and* religious. Yes, I am including religious in the invitation, something that the rural church should be an expert in—but she often sends the wrong message. We freak out about how the "sky is falling" with the "Spiritual But Not Religious" (SBNR) phenomenon. Our perception of SBNR is that rural residents are leaving the "religious" church behind in droves. In reality, we need to slow down enough to assess what is actually possible. For those of us familiar with the "Chicken Little" fable, you realize I just called us a bunch of chickens.

## SBNR

Richard stared into his empty coffee mug for a good 30 seconds before he spoke. "I'd have to say that I'm spiritual but not really religious." He paused as he looked up to make eye contact with me. "I believe, I really, truly believe . . . it just might not look like what you expect."

Richard's sincere description of his faith is a growing phenomenon in America, yet I am not convinced that we know what Richard's words truly mean. I am not all too sure that Richard really understands what the phrase "Spiritual But Not Religious" (SBNR) means.

Does SBNR mean that he believes in Jesus Christ as Lord and Savior but is skeptical of belonging to a church because of old wounds? Does it mean that he believes in a higher power or some sort of spiritual force out there but not Christianity? Does it mean that he is all about Jesus Christ and participating in his local church but wants to convey that faith is "a relationship but not religion," a born-again experience that is more than doing good works?

With the increasing identification of SBNR in rural America, the rural church needs to better understand what SBNR means, and how the church is an accomplice in the phenomenon.

## The Phenomenon

The percentage of Americans who self-ascribe as SBNR, spiritual but not religious, is continuing to grow. Over one quarter of Americans (27 percent) describe themselves in this way, which is an eight-percentage point rise since 2012. On the other hand, the percentage of Americans who describe themselves as religious and spiritual is declining, now representing less than half of Americans (48 percent), a nine-percentage point drop since 2012.[1] We see SBNR clearly manifest itself in our rural communities where many will self-identify as a Christian, or at least a God-fearer, but a shrinking number are likely to connect deeply with a church.

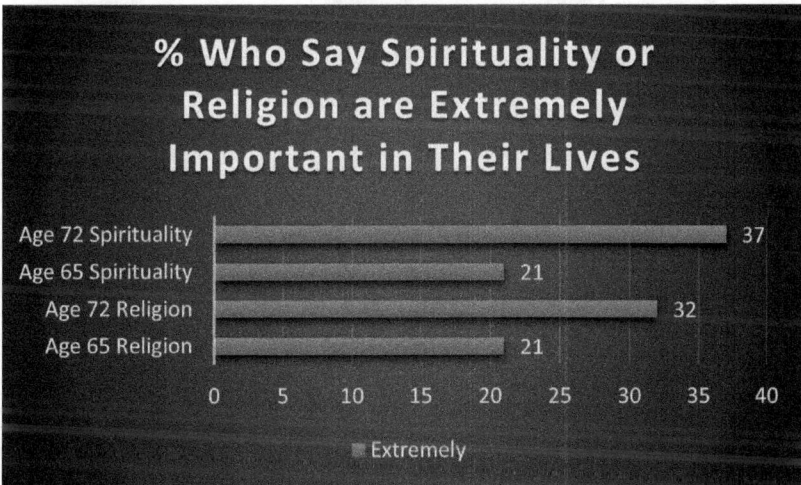

### % Who Say Spirituality or Religion are Extremely Important in Their Lives

| | |
|---|---|
| Age 72 Spirituality | 37 |
| Age 65 Spirituality | 21 |
| Age 72 Religion | 32 |
| Age 65 Religion | 21 |

Extremely

Spirituality and Religiousness Change with Age

1. Lipka and Gecewicz, "More Americans Now Say."

What might be even more surprising is that this change is happening among older Americans as well. We anticipate that people will become more engaged with faith as they age—it is a long-standing trend, but it is increasingly reflecting the focus on spirituality over religion. At age sixty-five, 21 percent of respondents stated that religion was extremely important in their life, rising to 32 percent of respondents by age seventy-two. That is an impressive rise, unless compared against spirituality. At age sixty-five, 21 percent of respondents stated that spirituality was extremely important in their lives, rising to 37 percent by age seventy-two.[2]

## WHAT DOES IT MEAN?

Richard said that he was spiritual but not religious. He did not readily offer up the specifics of what that means. That is the problem with the SBNR label. Social science research has increasingly framed "spiritual but not religious" (SBNR) as a growing phenomenon. The implicit and explicit message captured in this research is that SBNR is a movement toward privatized faith.[3] That cultural trend does not bode well for inviting people to church in our rural communities, if the trend is being defined correctly.

The root of SBNR points back to the intersection of believing and belonging—as people lean toward spirituality rather than religion, they maintain or increase in their self-ascribed belief, but no longer belong to a church. Grace Davie famously brought the modern phenomenon of SBNR to the forefront with the catch phrase of "believing without belonging."[4] One can believe in God but largely reject the church. Two questions emerge in response to the growing emphasis on SBNR: 1) are people consistent in

2. The Wisconsin Longitudinal Study (WLS) has followed one cohort since 1957, making it one of the longest continuous studies of its kind in the United States (Herd et al., "Cohort Profile," 36). The WLS has followed 1957 Wisconsin high school graduates through mail surveys, phone interviews, and in-person surveys over successive waves based on a random sample of 1/3 of the total graduates. Participants were born between 1938 and 1940 and 2/3 have continued to live in Wisconsin throughout the waves of study (Herd et al., "Cohort Profile," 34, 35). See Wisconsin Longitudinal Study (WLS), "Graduates, Siblings, and Spouses."

3. Herzog and Beadle, "Emerging Adult Religiosity and Spirituality," 1; Ammerman, "Spiritual But Not Religious?," 258; Murphy, "Beyond 'Religion' and 'Spirituality,'" 1–26.

4. Davie, *Religion in Britain Since 1945*; Davie, *Religion in Britain.*

what they mean when self-identifying as spiritual or religious, and 2) is the distinction between spiritual and religious truly binary?[5]

People are about as consistent in their use of the words "spiritual" and "religious" as they are in saying that the weather is "cool" or "warm." Think about how we use cool and warm—a hardy Midwesterner might think that sixty degrees is warm spring weather, while someone from the southern tip of Florida will think it is less than cool. There is also within-individual variability with these terms. That same Midwesterner will consider forty degrees to be warm weather in February, unless it is the temperature of their living room.

Clearly, there is variability of "warm" and "cool" which limits their usefulness as labels. The same is true for spiritual and religious. While someone might use the "Spiritual but not Religious" (SBNR) statement to say that they do not go to church, conservative Protestants might use that same SBNR phrase to emphasize that a personal relationship with Jesus Christ is necessary over cultural Christianity. The "religion" that these conservatives are separating themselves from is very different than the "religion" that the "none's" and "done's" are referring to.[6]

Even the word "believe" has radically different connotations. A Christian might use it as a means of talking about devout spirituality while a skeptic might use it as a way of describing superstition, which would still get lumped in as spirituality. Likewise, the word "belong" can represent a positive identity with a group, or in the opposite direction it can serve as a symbol of being trapped in an authoritarian structure where the individual loses their own voice.[7]

## SPIRITUAL AND RELIGIOUS

So SBNR is not a phrase with consistent meaning—but what can we as rural churches learn from the increasing use of this phrase? "Spiritual" consistently refers to a privatized experience. The word is to indicate what someone does on their own. At the same time, spiritual is not necessarily distinct from the religious group that the individual identifies with. An individual's privatized experience necessarily overlaps with the religious activity of a group.

5. Ammerman, "Spiritual But Not Religious?," 276.

6. Ammerman, "Spiritual But Not Religious?," 274–75.

7. Ammerman, "Spiritual But Not Religious?," 273.

"Religion" focuses on organized tradition. For Christians, this is generally some sort of reference to a local church. Yet, participation in the local church does not mean that the individual avoids privately oriented expressions.[8] Religion lacks authenticity without an accompanying "spiritual domain."[9]

Thus, there is not a binary distinction between spiritual and religion—they actually overlap, even with the different nuances that people give to these words. The key to note is that people experience different overlaps of religiosity and spirituality.[10] Some will attend worship services yet practice few spiritual disciplines in their home. Some will rarely attend a worship serve, yet fervently pray and consistently read their Bible.

The window of opportunity for the church is to invite people into an overlap of spiritual *and* religious. That is an opportunity that the church should be an expert in—but often sends the wrong message.

## WHAT SHOULD RURAL CHURCHES DO?

1. *Stop talking about only a privatized faith experience.* When we focus our gospel message as solely "Jesus and me" we send the clear message that Christian community is extra credit. Should it come as a surprise that people subsequently end up satisfied with the truncated experience of "Spiritual But Not Religious"? As much as we want to complain about people who do not regularly participate in church, we need to look at how we have invited them. Often, we have invited them into a privatized experience with God, and the only reason to join with other people is if they have a problem or difficult situation that needs to be worked through. This might be especially significant for rural churches plowing the hard ground of remnant Christendom where there is a need to push through the culture of American civil religion[11]—but we must not leave the blessing of organized religion behind as we call for personal renewal.

2. *Watch out for glow words.* When someone says that they "believe in Jesus" that might not mean what we think. The focus on spirituality

8. Streib et al., "'Spirituality' as Privatized Experience-Oriented Religion," 449. Streib et al., "Deconversion and 'Spirituality,'" 24.

9. Ammerman, "Spiritual But Not Religious?," 276.

10. Herzog and Beadle, "Emerging Adult Religiosity and Spirituality," 15.

11. Bellah, "Civil Religion in America," 1–21.

gives license to people to make their own religious framework without reference to what words and phrases have historically meant. Rather than just being irritated that someone is not attending a Bible Study or worship service, we should listen to what they say. When we start to understand what they actually mean by spirituality and like terms, we can better understand how to invite them. There is not a one-size-fits-all approach to SBNR.

And let's be honest. Glow words are especially prevalent in rural America. There is a great deal of God-fearing, at least God as Creator, but not necessarily an understanding of our need to submit to Jesus Christ as Savior and Lord. Rather than just assuming that people are going to reject the religious idea of Christian community, we need to peel back the layers and speak into places where words used do not line up with beliefs and behavior. Spiritual might not mean Christian.

3. *Invite into authentic ritual.* Some readers might be frustrated that this has not been a head on theological or ecclesiological attack on SBNR. There is plenty of fodder to make this possible. However, it does not seem likely that debate is going to be winsome to someone who has a negative impression of church. There is a need for experiential understanding rather than a battle of concepts. After all, the specifics of spiritual and religious are so messy, the likelihood of a fruitful debate of these terms is unlikely. We need to invite people into the experience of authentic ritual.

## Invite Them to Experience Religion: Authentic Ritual

Is this a counter-intuitive approach? Yes, inviting people into religion when it is increasingly cast in a negative light seems dubious at first. But it is a straight-on approach to addressing SBNR and the negative impact on churches.

Experience opens the door to grasping the beauty of religion once again—providing a taste of what the good surrounding the term actually is. The key is to avoid inviting someone to the wrong thing. Clearly, none of us want to invite someone to a staid experience which is so cold and ritualistic that someone's negative preconceptions of religion are reinforced.

At the same time, if we invite someone to a church function which is essentially a privatized spiritual experience, we have done the same. If we invite someone to an experience where they are within a group of people, but simply consume everything in their own bubble, there is no reason that they cannot have the same experience completely on their own.

We often turn the conversation at this point to fellowship and the importance of Christian community. That is good and right, but it often throws a therapeutic Christianity vibe. If you join the group, you will feel better, overcome something, grow deeper friendships. This is all true, but again casts the image of community as extra credit—if you want it.

Along with inviting into Christian fellowship, there is a need to invite into ritual.[12] Zoinks, for some of us that ritual word is scary, giving a picture of rote practices that are lifeless and lacking vibrancy. There are indications that "religious done's" who have left the church are especially responsive to invitations to opportunities where they can discover the significance of rituals that they associate with Christianity, such as the meaning of the Lord's Prayer or the context surrounding the Lord's Supper. They do not want a chaplaincy experience of being made comfortable, they want to be challenged with a new understanding or application, especially if it transforms their childhood religious socialization. Some success stories involve "low tradition" churches that start utilizing creeds and catechisms in the worship service. The success lays in explaining those traditional rituals and connecting them with Scripture and life application.[13]

The rural church has plenty of opportunity to invite. The question is if our invitation will feed into the Spiritual But Not Religious phenomenon, or if we will move towards a much-needed correction.

Our traditional toolbox is to run to one extreme or the other. On the one hand, we run to the religious extreme, and try to shoehorn people into attending something church oriented. We look at gathered worship or study as the only avenues to invite people into and overlook the opportunity to speak into the spiritual journey that someone is actually on. On the other hand, we can be so focused on the spiritual "just Jesus and me" approach that we miss the essential element of Christian community. One thing that the COVID season has been revealing is how anemic our encouragement of Christian community has been.

---

12. Swart, "Social Capital," 221–49; Swenson, *Society, Spirituality, and the Sacred*; Cilliers and Wepener, "Ritual and the Generation," 39–55.

13. Greene, "U.S. Baby Boomers." For examples of intentional use of liturgy see: Smith, *You Are What You Love: The Spiritual Power of Habit*; Kaemingk and Wilson, *Work and Worship*; Adams, *Gospel in a Handshake*.

# CHAPTER 10

# The Data

I F rural churches are going to most effectively reach rural residents, we need to know the most likely pathways that rural residents journey on to move toward increasing faith in Jesus Christ as Lord and Savior. In a qualitative study of rural residents from a variety of rural settings and denominations, I asked people who came to faith as adults to tell their story. The narrative that they shared through gentle promptings painted a picture of how they describe their transition from a place of no faith or nominal faith to a faith that includes self-identified changes in Christian religiosity.[1]

There is an overall pattern of baby boomer descriptions of religious change: they are most likely to describe their change in religiosity in terms of belonging. This has a significant impact on where we place our emphasis as rural churches ministering to rural adults.

## DESCRIPTION PATTERNS OF BELONGING, BEHAVING, AND BELIEVING

Rural residents do not follow a given sequence when it comes to religious change. There is not some sort of formula where a baby boomer starts to belong, then they believe, and finally begin to behave as a Christian. We are now going to take a closer look at the data behind the Venn diagram that clarifies the summary that believing was by far the least referenced change

1. Participant overview reminder: A total of 50 interviews were conducted where the residential context was between zones 2 and 9 of the USDA ERS Rural Urban Continuum Code (RUCC) in the North Central Region of the United States. In the end, 31 baby boomer interviews and 19 pastor or ministry leader interviews were utilized.

of religiosity, belonging was the most referenced change, and behaving was in between.

The diagram captures a few elements that we will see in the findings. Belonging really stood out in the stories as the most common descriptor—but it was also interconnected with behaving and believing. These descriptors are not mutually exclusive. For instance, the intersection of belonging to a church and expectations of moral Christian behavior are tightly interwoven. While there are points of intersection among the three descriptors of change in religiosity, they also have unique features. Hence, from the vantage point of rural adults themselves, change in religiosity involves all three descriptors, with an emphasis on belonging.

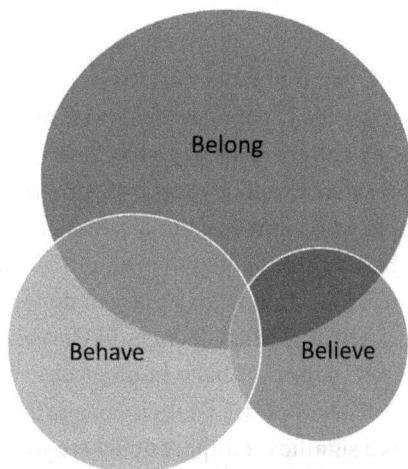

**Venn Diagram of Religiosity: Belong, Behave, Believe**

Not only was belonging the most common descriptor, but it was also the most intensely expressed. Based on coding and spreadsheet analysis, belonging was described as a significant change (4.6), behaving was moderate (4.2), and believing was less than moderate (3.7).[2]

---

2. I tracked believing, belonging, and behaving through coding, as well as a five-point scale analysis tracked in a spreadsheet. The 3 indicated no change, 4 indicated moderate change, and 5 indicated significant change.

## Significance of Change in Religiosity

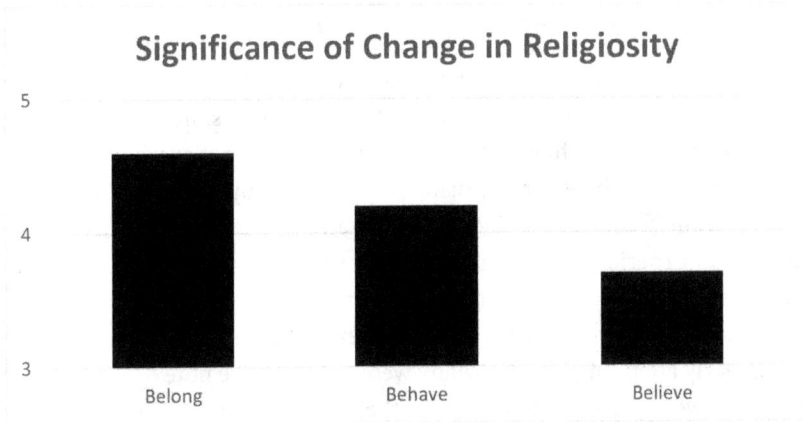

Self-identified Change in Religiosity Based on Intensity of Expression

On the one hand, these differences in frequency and intensity of religiosity descriptors make sense. Since many rural adults have been religiously socialized, it stands to reason that many would not identify significant changes in beliefs. When it comes to belonging, since many went through a time of disaffiliation or attended in a nominal way in early life, it once again stands to reason that this change would be significant. Finally, the moderate change in behavior also lines up with expectations that many would change their lifestyle or personal spiritual disciplines as they reconsidered their faith.

While these overall findings might be expected, the specifics used in describing belonging, behaving, and believing offer insights that were not well documented in previous literature. We now turn to these specific findings to hear what baby boomers share about their religiosity change.

## CHANGE IN BELIEVING

Rural adults are more likely to describe their faith transitions as a process rather than a light switch event. Even descriptions of conversion tended to be more season oriented than instantaneous. As we examine the data, we need to recognize that these stories should impact how we should approach evangelism with rural adults.

## Conversion

The importance of conversion experience was mentioned by twelve of the thirty-one participants. These conversations of conversion circled around a specific event—for church traditions that practice believer's baptism, it often involved their water baptism. As described by a number of those coming from a very low religious socialization in childhood, their adult conversion experience was "the best day of my life." The specific day and setting is remembered with detail along with what they felt.

Discussions about conversion were very different for those who grew up regularly attending church. Many were able to make note of the process that they went through as a part of their "conversion" in their youth—whether it was baptism or public confession of faith, but few saw this as a significant part of their spiritual journey. In fact, four individuals from fundamentalist traditions cited their conversion experience as very negative in relation to their overall faith experience. They felt that they received a skewed picture of what faith was about, which kept them spiritually off track for decades. All four saw their youth conversion experience as a moral equation: "you had to be good to get into heaven."

## Intensity and Power Experiences

Although most do not point to a conversion event as the key in their change of beliefs, all point to seasons of life where significant changes in religiosity took place. Rather than a singular event in which their religious beliefs changed or grew, most primarily identify with seasons of change. This slower, life course experience included both absorbing new beliefs and raising the priority of certain religious beliefs.

For instance, Betty spoke about her belief of biblical forgiveness. She "always" embraced the importance of forgiveness, but if it was inconvenient or difficult, the value was lower than exacting revenge. Over a specific season in her life where she went through a difficult divorce, the value of biblical forgiveness increased dramatically. Again, she would not say that her belief changed, but the value of it did, to the point that her behavior was subsequently altered. The change in belief was not instantaneous, but a process that took in the season of divorce along with previous life experiences to make biblical forgiveness a primary value rather than secondary.

Again, most indicated the change in beliefs as slower seasonal changes that were more focused on raising the value of their belief rather than a sudden change. What is significant is that nineteen of the thirty-one attributed a sense of intensity to this change in belief. Although there was not necessarily a "conversion experience" that took place, there was a sense of intensity, whether it was through prayer, a sense of God's nearness, a physical lightness from a burden removed, or, as nearly one-third identified, a power experience.

Power experiences ranged from stories about release from demonic oppression to physical healing to hearing God's audible voice to interpreted dreams to visions to miraculous protection. Of the thirty-one interviews, ten specifically cited a power experience as a part of their change in beliefs. What is fascinating is that only three of the stories are directly connected to an instantaneous conversion experience. Most of the power experiences were a catalyst for a longer-term shift in belief. Even for those who talked about the power experience as a part of their conversion experience, they still painted the event as more of a catalyst for long term change.

For instance, Silas was in a tavern mentally working through his life struggles and also identifying the addictions that were impacting him. Out of desperation, he prayed to God—something he had not done in earnest for decades. He instantly felt a release from his addictions and a physical lightness with his struggles in perspective. He clearly identifies this as a power encounter in which he experienced significant change. At the same time, his actual change in belief was much slower—there was a season of spiritual journeying before he committed his life to Jesus Christ as Lord and Savior.

One caveat to this discussion is that intensity and power experiences were hardly mentioned by people who remained connected to a church throughout their lives. This group expressed little overall change in beliefs, and what did take place, was not a part of a dramatic season of experiences.

## Discipleship and Exemplars

Given that belief change took place over a considerable period of time for most of the interviewees, it is intuitive that an oft cited change surrounds discipleship. The idea of "following Jesus" or learning more about what it means to be a Christian ranked high in importance. In fact, twenty-eight of the thirty-one participants indicated that an element of discipleship has been moderately or extremely important in their change of beliefs or valuing of beliefs.

The importance of discipleship is a reflection of people who are now orthodox in their belief and practice—in many ways discipleship is an anticipated practice of Christians. The benefit of interviews is that we can move beyond quantitative analysis and examine qualitative elements. Interviewees not only spoke a great deal about discipleship and specific areas of growth, but they also conveyed their stories with emotion. They indicated that discipleship and the change in their valuing of certain beliefs was of significant importance that continues to impact them.

A caveat to the discussion about changes in valuing beliefs is the impact of exemplars—people who serve as role models of faithful living. Exemplars were cited by twenty of the thirty-one participants as positive influences for change in beliefs. The role of exemplars once again points to the impact of change over seasons. Individuals interact with and are influenced by exemplars over periods of time, although the type of exemplars varies by person.

Some focused on exemplars from their youth who continue to impact their lives, even though the exemplar has long since passed. If anything, the impact of the exemplar may be even more significant as the individual may now be similar in age to the exemplar when she or he influenced them. For others, especially those without childhood exemplars, many referenced their pastor or small group leader as a key exemplar who has dramatically shaped them.

The role of exemplars in discipleship provides a bridge to belonging—exemplars and even the broader discipleship process is something that takes place in community. We now turn to specific references to belonging that baby boomers consistently mentioned in the interviews.

## Change in Belonging

### Process

As previously noted, belonging is the most identified change in religiosity overall. Nearly all (twenty-six of thirty-one) told a story about the process of their change in belonging. Of interest is that every male (fourteen of fourteen) told a story that moderately or significantly referenced their process of belonging, while twelve of the seventeen women referenced a story of process of belonging.

There was an oft repeated process. First, they began with a sense of emotional distance from church. They either had disaffiliated from regular participation, or they were dissatisfied with their church even though they were physically attending. Second, they were facing some sort of catalyst for being spiritually sensitive. Third, a friend or family member invited them to attend church. The invitation usually came from someone they knew who was attending a church. For some it was an invitation from a lifelong friend. For others it was their adult child who invited them to join them. Other than those who remained with the same church, only three were not invited to "try out" a church.

## Baby Boomer References to Belonging Process

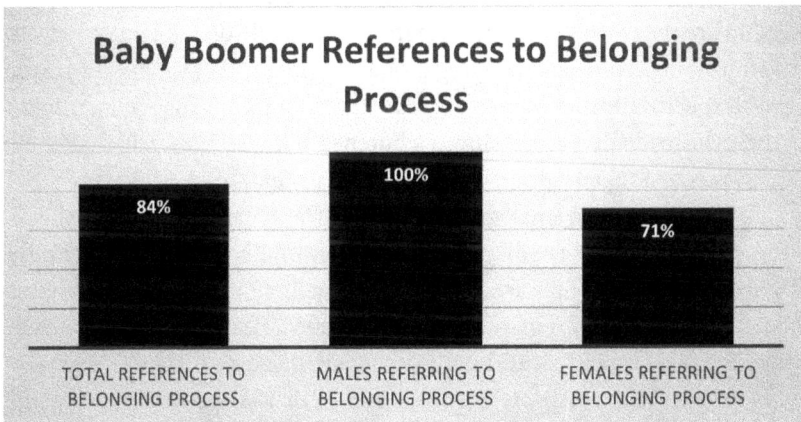

Baby Boomer References to Belonging Process

### Worship Setting and Small Group

We now move into examining what rural residents specifically identify as their primary belonging point. When it comes to the weekly worship service, twenty-four of the thirty-one expressed that their routine participation has moderately or significantly impacted their religiosity over recent years. When considering participation in small groups, twenty-five of the thirty-one shared how their faith was moderately or significantly impacted. An interesting caveat is that the impact of worship settings and small group settings do not necessarily overlap.

All thirty-one interviewed baby boomers expressed that either the worship setting or a small group had impacted their spiritual life over recent years: eighteen shared stories that demonstrated the impact of both worship and small group settings, seven highlighted small groups but not the worship setting, while six referenced worship but not the small group. There is clearly more than one path to a sense of belonging, and there are also some patterns to observe.

When it comes to valuing the worship setting, those who spent their childhood years in a conservative church setting where weekly worship attendance was expected and highlighted are most likely to find significance in worship during their later years. 95 percent of those who remained in a conservative church identified worship as significant.

Baby boomers who experienced deep religious socialization in weekly worship are those who identified the importance of worship rituals as well. The impact of sermons, of congregational singing, and of corporate prayer were all specifically highlighted as important and significant. In fact, some of these individuals even changed churches because they felt that their church was no longer putting enough emphasis on traditional worship.

When it comes to small groups, an important question arises—what is it that people mean by small group? For some, small group is a Bible Study of fifteen or fewer people where there is a facilitator of discussion rather than a formal teacher. For others, small group refers to a smaller group where the Bible is referenced, but life issues are discussed. There were references to even more intimate groups, of three or four people who organically came together to process life together. For some, the catalyst for this type of group was grief surrounding the death of a loved one.

Regardless of the exact size of the small group, there was an important distinction apart from the worship service. The worship service was seen as a formal ministry of the church. Most of the small groups referenced in interviews were seen as informal—either tangentially connected to the church or sponsored by a para-church ministry. The small group offered a different entry point to belonging than the worship service—not just in content, but also because it was perceived as a safe place.

Many of those who came back to church through small group attendance cite the key aspect of a safe place to process their faith and life concerns. Becky shared that a friend leading a small group "is the one that really got me involved in the Bible study because she asked me several times to come." Notice that there were repeated invitations, and also care for safe place, "I was real uncomfortable . . . because people think . . . I know a lot about the Bible and I really don't . . . [it's] very surprising to a lot of people that that I didn't know more than I know."

As shared above, some adults are very self-conscious about their Bible knowledge. Some referred to themselves as "elementary school students" when it comes to their self-image of biblical literacy beyond Christmas and Easter. Others desperately desired for a safe space to share their struggles with personal health, with losses in their life, concern about children and grandchildren, or maybe even a place to celebrate the good things that are happening, such as more time in their schedule.

One desire for safe space circled around long term hurts that baby boomers have been unable to share for most of their lives. Multiple participants talked about how it has not been until the last ten years that they have felt free to share some of their painful life stories. Some had hidden disfunction in their homes (childhood as well as their own) until they found a small group that they trusted. Others had never spoken about their financial struggles, mental illness, or addictions, out of fear of being judged. While many favorably expressed opportunity to belong to a small group, some still hoped for more. During the interviews, there were stories shared that were prefaced by "I have never told anyone this." It became clear that some baby boomers are searching for even more safe spaces where they can belong in order to share the hardest portion of their stories, from a secret abortion to hidden infidelity to participation in the occult.

Our rural churches desperately need to intentionally provide safe places rather than assume they exist with any small group that gathers. Leader training is essential to provide the right conversational pauses and to actively build trust among group members.

## Social, Friend and Family, Volunteering

There are a number of connections that create a sense of belonging. There is general social support provided by the church, especially in times of need. Zach spoke at length about how the church members rallied around him and his wife when she went through a significant illness soon after they started attending the church. From providing meals to helping with transportation to distant doctor appointments, the church filled a tremendous need. Of the thirty-one interviews, twenty-two provided significant stories about how their church had provided support that went beyond meeting physical needs, and encouraged them through a sense of spiritual kinship.

The specific role of friends and family in the church was moderate to very significant to twenty-seven of the thirty-one participants. Many of these friends and family were the catalyst who invited the baby boomer back to church. Some mentioned children and grandchildren who asked them to come to church; for Thad it was a sibling.

For Bob, belonging was through farming friendships. A group of three farmers had been friends for years. All three attended church regularly and all three felt open to talk about their faith in conversation. One friend was very outspoken about his faith. Another friend quietly lived out his faith but clearly displayed a sense of nearness to God that was foreign to the farmer who was interviewed. Over time, Bob became more disenchanted with his church experience and asked the quiet friend about his faith. Through subsequent conversations, Bob began attending the same church as his quiet friend. This friend not only served as Bob's catalyst to join the church, but also was an exemplar and encourager to Bob as he grew in his sense of belonging within the church.

Those who grew up in the church but became religiously indifferent expressed the most impact from friends and family. Those who had remained regular church attenders throughout their adult years shared by far the least about impact of family and friends. Most likely, these long-term church goers did not feel the impact of belonging from a champion within the church since they already felt a sense of ownership when it came to belonging to a church.

Volunteering was another route toward belonging[3] in which twenty-one of the thirty-one participants cited stories of spiritual growth through volunteering. Those who had regularly attended church at times in their life were the most likely to reference volunteering: fourteen of the sixteen cited volunteering as moderately to very impactful on their spiritual growth.

Volunteering of significance included food closets, community renewal initiatives, and mission trips. Far and away the most likely place for volunteering was in youth ministry. Many shared stories of how they enjoy learning alongside the kids, and also how they can provide these kids with spiritual experiences that were lacking in their own childhood. The strong

---

3. Volunteering is a prime example of the intersection of behaving and belonging. While volunteering is an indication of change in behavior, it is also a marker of increased belonging. The volunteering findings were placed within belonging since the volunteering was described as a group endeavor more than a personal behavior change.

sense of belonging associated with volunteering came through giving and receiving. It was very important to these baby boomers that they were not only receiving ministry from the church, but that they also had the opportunity to invest their own skills, talents, and abilities in ministry.

Baby boomers who were not drawn by volunteering tended to be those who had dabbled in quasi-Christian experiences. Not a single individual with this experience expressed the importance of volunteering in their description of religious change. They shared stories of how they had been misguided in the past and heavily volunteered for a variety of causes that in the end were not purposeful. Coming out of those experiences, these individuals tend to be less expectant of experiencing growth through volunteering.

## Composite View of Belonging

The interviews provide a snapshot of how churches provide belonging. When it comes to relationships, social support as well as friends and family matter.

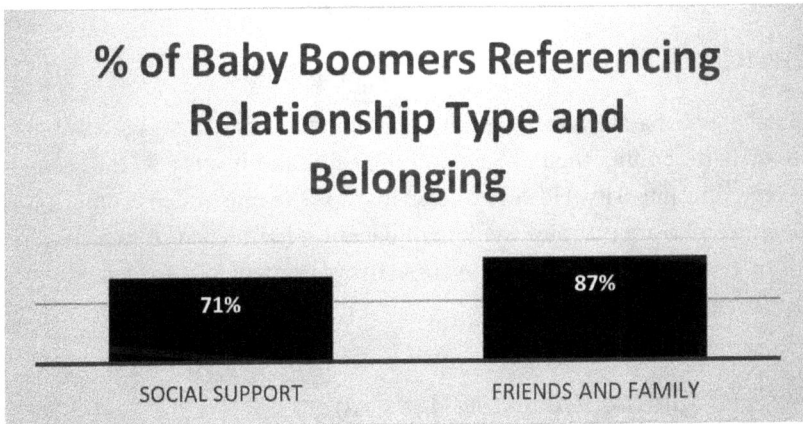

**% of Baby Boomers Referencing Relationship Type and Belonging**

| | |
|---|---|
| 71% | 87% |
| SOCIAL SUPPORT | FRIENDS AND FAMILY |

Percent of Baby Boomers Referencing Relationship Type and Belonging

The settings offered were important as well. We observed the impact of worship settings, small group opportunities, and also service group opportunities through volunteering.

## % of Baby Boomers Referencing Group Settings and Belonging

| | | |
|---|---|---|
| 77% | 81% | 68% |
| WORSHIP | SMALL GROUP | SERVICE GROUP |

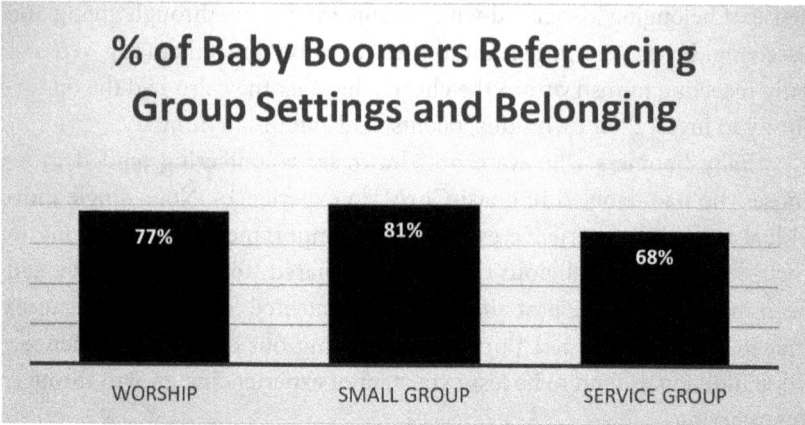

Percent of Baby Boomers Referencing Group Settings and Belonging

Now that we have walked through elements of believing and belonging, we turn to behaving. For the most part, however, the changes in believing, belonging, and behaving took place across a similar season and did not follow a set sequence.

## CHANGE IN BEHAVING

Changes in behaving was the second most common descriptor used by baby boomers describing their change in religiosity, and it was also the second in regard to intensity. However, behaving was the most intense descriptor for those who at one point were unaffiliated or disaffiliated from a church. All of those who at one point were actively nonreligious expressed very significant change in behavior.

### Personal Spiritual Disciplines and Prayer

Personal spiritual disciplines include: prayer, Scripture reading, biblical meditation, fasting, devotions, and other orthodox Christian practices that are done within one's home. Through the telling of their stories, twenty-six of the thirty-one baby boomers expressed moderate to significant changes in at least one of their personal spiritual disciplines. Stories were shared how individuals rarely or never read Scripture or prayed at home and began to do so in early old age. Specific practices were shared about how they make this a routine, such as Thomas talking about praying out loud with a cup of coffee first thing in the morning.

Many referenced what they now see as a misuse of spiritual disciplines in the past. They would engage in a variety of spiritual disciplines for various seasons in their lives depending on the issue or challenge that they were facing, and then move on once the problem was over. Thad had faced a series of health challenges over the years and was in the practice of praying until the particular season was over. Finally, when his diabetes became so severe that an appendage needed to be amputated, his use of prayer changed. Accepting that his prayer was not simply to maintain his current health status, but to adjust to a new normal, he recognized an open door to a new manner of praying. As he made a public profession of faith in Jesus Christ through baptism during this time, he also embraced a prayer life that went beyond his own need in the moment. He began to search out dialog with God.

While some start practices that they had never consistently done before, such as Scripture reading, others spoke about finding new meaning or experience in practices that they had given up on. The discipline that was most often mentioned was prayer. In fact, twenty of the thirty-one interviewees specifically mentioned moderate to significant changes in their prayer experience.

Based on the stories, it seems as though these individuals link back to the prayer practices that they grew up with (or at least how they remember them) and see their current prayer life as a continuation of that pattern. Religious socialization made a significant impact in this regard—those who were religiously indifferent in their childhood now observe significant change in prayer practices while those who grew up in the church and then left church for a period of time during their adult years do not see much difference.

## Lifestyle

While a vast majority of baby boomers in this study identified behavior change with an increase in the practice or experience of personal spiritual disciplines, eighteen of the thirty-one shared stories of moderate to significant change in lifestyle. Only two of those who experienced a change in lifestyle did not express a change in personal spiritual practices.

The change in lifestyle ranged from addressing an addiction to curtailing cursing to becoming a more personable individual. One item that was listened for in this section of the research was a change away from cohabitation. In previous interviews with baby boomers,[4] I had found that a number of them were living with a "significant other" when they experienced a change in religiosity, and part of their behavior shift was either getting married or changing living arrangements to live separately. While listening for this possibility during this study, only two expressed a change away from cohabitation.

A more significant shift in lifestyle surrounded charity: six of the thirty-one individuals shared a change in their financial giving to charities. Although the total number is relatively small, these six shared stories of how significant the shift was for them. For Ian, a very successful scientist, he found charity to be a freeing and significant change in his behavior. Rather than his career and legacy as an end in itself, he saw himself as part of a grander plan and purpose, in which part of his role was to contribute financially to others.

Another shift in lifestyle surrounded forgiveness: ten of the participants shared stories of a dramatic change in their practice of forgiveness. Some shared stories where they needed to forgive someone who had wronged them in the past, but they had held onto the situation through bitterness. Others shared stories where they needed to humbly approach someone to ask for forgiveness because of a wrong that they had committed—sometimes even years ago. Again, while this is just under one-third of the group, the impact was especially poignant for the individuals sharing these stories. Likewise, it is important to note that seven of the ten sharing forgiveness stories were women.

## Coping Mechanisms

A number of people shared stories that directly pointed to a change in the practice of spiritual disciplines or alteration in lifestyle as a coping mechanism. Twenty-seven of the thirty-one participants shared stories that made it clear that their behavior was changed in response to a stress in life.

---

4. Greene, *Hunger to Belong.*

## % of Baby Boomers Describing Type of Behavior Change

84%

58%

SPIRITUAL DISCIPLINES    LIFESTYLE

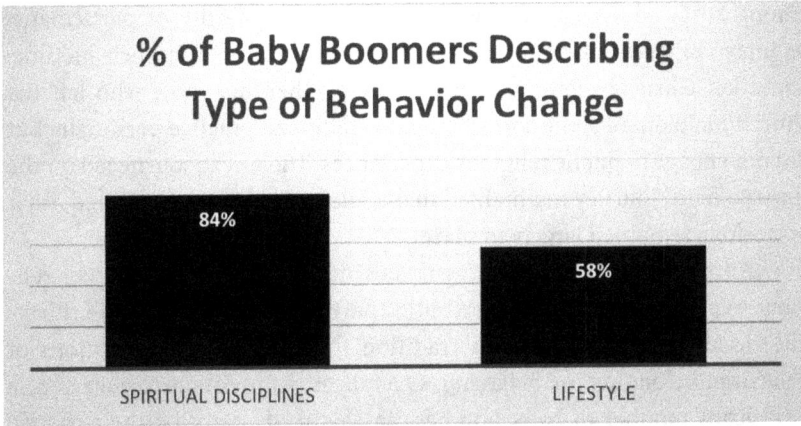

Percent of Baby Boomers Describing Type of Behavior Change

Within the two broad categories of behavioral change of spiritual disciplines and lifestyle, there were three specific behaviors presented in interviews: prayer, charity, and forgiveness.

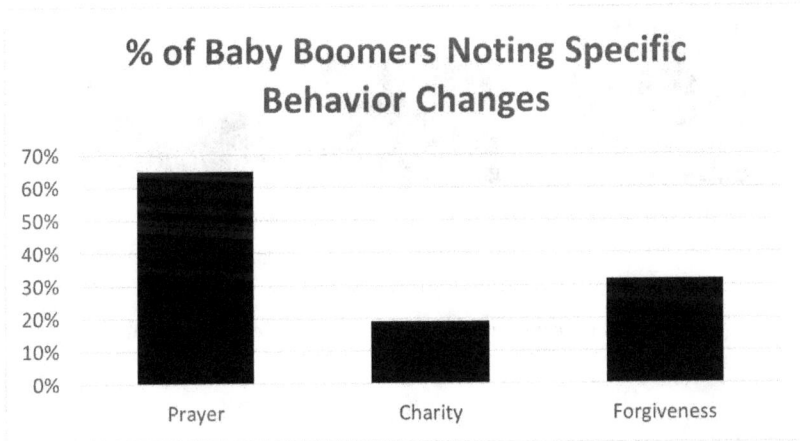

## % of Baby Boomers Noting Specific Behavior Changes

70%
60%
50%
40%
30%
20%
10%
0%

Prayer    Charity    Forgiveness

Percent of Baby Boomers Noting Specific Behavior Change

## PATHWAYS

In addition to the overall pattern of frequency and intensity of religiosity descriptions, research revealed important pathways to be mindful of among rural adults connecting to a church. A majority of participants (eighteen of thirty-one) had left the church at some point in their lifetime. Some left Christian faith and practice altogether, but most who left the church maintained some sort of religious faith and practice personally but did not engage in public religious experiences. Those who journeyed on the "private faith" journey maintained that while their orthopraxy waned, their orthodoxy remained largely in place.

Another interesting pathway is moving to a church with higher religious expectations. Over 60 percent of participants (twenty of the thirty-one) identified that they left a tradition that had lower expectations of believing, belonging, or behaving. Overall, it is important to note that a significant number of baby boomers in this study describe their change in religiosity through the lens of a different church experience later in life.

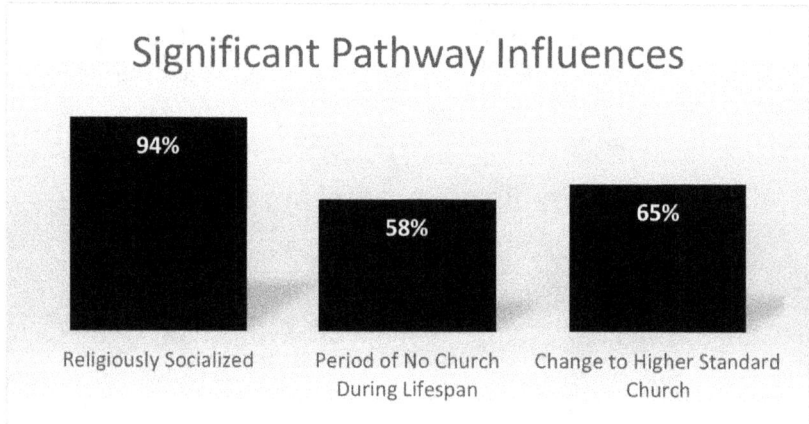

## Significant Pathway Influences

| Religiously Socialized | Period of No Church During Lifespan | Change to Higher Standard Church |
|:---:|:---:|:---:|
| 94% | 58% | 65% |

**Significant Influences on Religiosity Change Over the Life Span**

## CONCLUSION

Overall, baby boomers expressed change in religiosity in terms of belonging. While behaving received considerable attention as a change in religiosity during early old age, it was not at the same magnitude as changes in belonging. Believing was by far the least referenced change when it comes to early old age changes in religiosity and is more of a change in valuing the beliefs than in ascribing to new beliefs.

We observed that there is not a set sequence between believing, belonging, and behaving. When it comes to believing, discipleship is a leading marker that reflects a seasonal rather than instantaneous change. We observed that belonging contains critical reference points: the worship setting, the small group, service opportunities, and relational connections. Behaving was most described as a change in lifestyle, altered practice of spiritual disciplines, or a combination of the two. Often times these behavior changes were linked to the need for coping with something that was beyond the baby boomer's control.

Let's come back to our toolbox discussion. When it comes to ministry to rural adults, belonging is a tool that we should be using. Which belonging tool might be the appropriate question—is my church offering opportunities to belong in various group sizes and formats? When it comes to believing, we need to ask if the only tool we are wielding is the expectation of a Road to Damascus conversion, or if we are more prepared for the process of a Road to Emmaus season of conversion. The data would point to the idea that among rural adults, our evangelism should be much more relationship oriented and process sensitive. When it comes to behaving, we likewise need to listen well for the changes that people are being nudged toward through discipleship. Now, we will take one final look at belonging with specifics to consider in our own rural context.

# CHAPTER 11

# Belonging Application

W E will now examine attributes of three identified points of belonging: 1) the worship setting, 2) small groups, and 3) service groups. Each of these points of belonging offer important pull factors to baby boomers: safe places, challenge over chaplaincy, informal design, storytelling, and relationships, captured in the following chart.

| | Safe Places | Challenge Over Chaplaincy | Informal Design | Storytelling | Relationships |
|---|---|---|---|---|---|
| Worship | Trust | Authentic Ritual | Norms | Narrative | Linking |
| Small Groups | Thick Trust | Issue Based | Horizontal Reciprocity | Sense Making | Bonding |
| Service Groups | Thin Trust | Religious | Vertical Reciprocity | Testimony | Bridging |

Points of Belonging Intersecting with Church Pull Factors

## POINTS OF BELONGING

The findings indicate that the church must be intentional in her design to provide opportunities to belong within three specific spaces: corporate worship, small groups, and service groups. Churches offering these spaces are not unique—but how the belonging opportunities are intentionally offered to adults makes the difference. Each of these spaces offer opportunities for individuals to interact with others, to participate in certain ways, and to find fulfilling connection with others that leads to a unique sense of belonging.[1] When a baby boomer is in the church sanctuary with a large group of people for weekly worship, she has certain relational expectations, but when at a coffee shop for a small group gathering the expected interactions are much different.[2] The goal is to go beyond merely offering these spaces but to intentionally design these spaces.

## Worship Setting

The worship setting refers to the weekly gathering of a church which typically includes congregational singing, praying, announcements, and a sermon. This is the ritual gathering of the large group that generates a patterned identity. When asked about religious observance, the answer is "I go to Church X," which is the worship service, the public marker of belonging.

## Small Groups

The small group refers to a discussion-based gathering of people for the specific purpose of supporting one another, often including an element of Bible study and prayer. The most effective small groups tended to be twelve or less people and were "separate" from the church. Belonging to these small groups did not require a commitment to the church. In fact, the small groups eliciting the greatest sense of belonging were purposefully distanced from church structure. Baby boomers who had previously been disappointed by church experience felt much more welcome in "trying out" belonging to a small group that was overtly Christian, but not church structured.

## Service Groups

Service groups are larger than small groups and have a different function. Service groups are activity oriented and seek to meet the needs of others.

1. Myers, *Search to Belong*, 39; Hall, *Hidden Dimension*, 1. A great deal of the proxemics-based literature includes four groups in which there are also intimate groups, generally consisting of two or three people. I have included intimate groups as a subset of small groups.

2. McNeal, "Missional Communities—European Style," 47.

These are groups that undertake community rehabilitation projects while others go together on a short-term mission trip. There is a critical mass of people to accomplish the work. These groups are also fluid. While small groups tend to have expectations of people routinely attending, service groups are porous for people to simply commit to completing an individual project.

## SAFE SPACES

With intentional design, each of the group sizes can provide safe spaces for adults who have a growing desire for belonging while compensating for age-related losses. In order for mature adults to be vulnerable with their questions generated by health concerns, death of a loved one, concerns about children/grandchildren, or the life change brought on by retirement there must be a safe space to belong. The baby boomers in this study indicated that they left churches without safe spaces and connected with churches where they felt safe processing their life story. Sadly, the odds are against safe spaces for the elderly. Remember that in one study 90 percent of the elderly felt marginalized in their own church at times.[3]

There is another side to safe spaces to consider—baby boomers may be reengaging in church as a relative spiritual novice. Baby boomers have potentially had a life that is rich with experience, perhaps even corporate, financial, and status success, yet, they are now entering into a setting where they may be spiritually impoverished in relation to people much younger than they are.[4] Ministry practitioners should not assume or expect baby boomers will be familiar with Christian teachings and be biblically literate.

## Worship Setting

The weekly worship service provides a context for developing trust necessary for the "feel" of safe space.[5] Trustworthiness[6] is where we give other

---

3. Rolph et al., "What Churches May Have."

4. Kersten, interview by author.

5. The general safe space discussion builds from a broad definition of social capital which "refers to the norms and networks that enable people to act collectively" (Woolcock and Narayan 2000, 226; Woolcock, "Place of Social Capital," 70).

6. Coleman, "Social Capital," 102; Putnam, *Bowling Alone*, 136; Paxton, "Is Social Capital Declining?," 98.

people "the benefit of the doubt." We assume that people will be honest and are safe to engage with. This is not broad-based gullibility, but a general willingness to engage with others.[7] Practicing worship service rituals in community influences the level of trust and social bonding.

My findings have indicated that trust with "others" can be limited though. As we will see more in later chapters, community "natives" versus "non-natives" and other clear "in-group" versus "out-group" patterns are in place without intentionality in the rural setting. Hence, attention must be paid to trustworthiness as both "thick trust" and "thin trust," which can take place in small groups and service groups accordingly.

## SMALL GROUPS

Thick trust connects with the rural ideal. This trust refers to our willingness to work with people whom we know well and have shared relationships with over time.[8] The "thickness" refers to the layers that have developed due to mutual vulnerability and shared concerns. Participants in this research highlighted the importance of thick trust—people in their small groups had experienced similar losses and also consistently listened to personal sharing with compassion. Some baby boomers referenced leaving a small group because the group could not be trusted with personal information or expressions of emotion. The existence of the small group was not sufficient; there also needed to be thick trust. At the same time, thick trust is not enough on its own. The presence of rural "out groups" requires intentionality in breaking down barriers that arise from only thick trust.

## SERVICE GROUPS

When it comes to creating space for returning baby boomers to experience belonging in churches, there is a need to build thin trust. Thick trust will develop with time as relationships are formed, but initial steps toward belonging will require a culture of thin trust—which can come through service groups. Thin trust refers to our willingness to work with people that we do not know well—more along the lines of acquaintance than friend.

7. Putnam, *Bowling Alone*, 136. See also Peddle, "Rural Anglicanism in Newfoundland," 21.

8. Putnam, *Bowling Alone*, 136.

The willingness to work with the "generalized other" is the key element of thin trust.[9]

Service groups provide this sense of introductory "thin trust" by bringing people together for a specific purpose. The interaction through shared work allows for some trust to form across a large group of people. This is important for adults who may be unsure about committing to a church—they can begin to trust people without tremendous vulnerability on their part while also not being tied to the group beyond the length of the service project.

Overall, trust is an underdeveloped opportunity for churches. Baby boomers are longing for safe places to belong. Throughout the interviews, comments surrounding unresolved pain emerged from statements such as, "I did not have a safe place to address this issue from childhood until I met with a counselor a few years ago," to the statement, "I have never told anyone one this before, but . . ." The role of shame is significant both in the church setting and in the rural subculture—shame will curtail belonging by default when intentional trust is absent.

## CHALLENGE OVER CHAPLAINCY

Older adults express frustration that programs and activities are consistently designed for the frail, ill, and homebound without considering possible contributions that the elderly can make through ministry activity. The refined sense of belonging that older adults yearn for is captured in the following summary:

> They argued for 'challenge not chaplaincy.' Many wrote that older people want to be 'used' in the church, and want to be asked to do more. But there was a fear that offering to help might lead to rejection.[10]

The hunger for challenge is all the more present as baby boomers enter into retirement in relatively good health, have a predilection for purposeful service, and also possess gifts, talents, and abilities that they are now looking to invest in blessing future generations. Baby boomers are not simply looking for therapeutic religion to make themselves feel better, they want

---

9. Putnam, *Bowling Alone*, 136.

10. Mills et al., "Listening and Enabling," 54. This particular study utilized British participants, but has clear parallels with the North American research of this book.

something to invest in. Yet, the invitation to participate in a challenge must be nuanced. If the church only receives help in predetermined frameworks rather than taking people's gifts, talents, and abilities into account, that is hardly "ministry with" the baby boomer. The churches intentionally inviting baby boomers did not tell them to simply do jobs already there; they recognized that "filling a spot" is "not really finding our place."[11]

## WORSHIP SETTING

Baby boomers found refreshing challenge through worship services that offered authentic rituals. Many expressed that they had sat through enough boring sermons and meaningless traditions. Baby boomers were drawn to sermons that were direct and applicable, yet clearly rooted in Scripture. They also highlighted the importance of discovering the significance of rituals—the meaning of the Lord's Prayer, the context surrounding the Lord's Supper. They did not want a chaplaincy experience of being made comfortable, they wanted to be challenged with a new understanding or application, especially if it transformed their childhood religious socialization. One success story involved a "low tradition" church utilizing creeds and catechisms in the worship service due to the tradition of many baby boomers. The success lay in explaining those traditional rituals and connecting them with Scripture and life application.

## SMALL GROUPS

The challenge desired in small groups focused on issue-based discussion. The small groups that opened the door to belonging dealt with death of loved ones, divorce, troubled children and grandchildren, financial issues, as well as personal health decline. The small groups were not about a single issue only—but they were flexible and contained enough thick trust that allowed for processing age-related losses.

## SERVICE GROUPS

The service groups that were most referenced had a clearly religious element to them. While the project itself may have been focused on a physical

11. Myers, *Organic Community*, 53.

improvement, there were Bible studies or times of prayer that were specifically directed to participants. Likewise, a number of interviews referenced the fact that they were expected to get outside their comfort zone in "living out" their faith. The challenge to publicly display their faith through action or spoken word was appealing since they could try it out during the duration of the project, and then decide if they really wanted that to be part of their identity or not. The chance to "try on" overt Christian behavior helped many to decide to seek out more opportunities.

## INFORMAL DESIGN

A recurring theme of baby boomer interviews focused on organizational informality and avoidance of unnecessary structure. At the same time, the churches successful in drawing in baby boomers displayed forms of implicit design that maintain a functioning organization.

### WORSHIP SETTING

Weekly worship is a place where effective churches provided clear norms. The worship service is the place where common convictions are rehearsed through spoken words and rituals. Not only are norms presented, but their corresponding sanctions are introduced as well. Elements of the worship service explain the penalty when the rules are broken, which is a critical component to social value-oriented baby boomers. Sanctions also provide organizational structure: there is a systematic way to maintain peace and protect against aggressive behaviors along with penalties for violating the rules. Safe spaces require enforcement of the rules.[12] The churches successful in providing safe places for baby boomers were effective in developing norms and sanctions as a part of their church culture.

### SMALL GROUPS

Horizontal reciprocity is something of a favor in the bank.[13] The most effective small groups provide a context of generalized reciprocity—I will do something for you now, and though I do not expect anything from you

---

12. Portes, "Social Capital," 10.
13. Putnam, *Bowling Alone*, 20.

down the road, I can be confident that someone else will do something similar. The idea is that a group of people are operating under the general terms of the Golden Rule—we do not have specifics about who will return the action in like kind, but we are confident that someone from the group will treat us in like kind as time goes on.[14] Small groups have this implicit design—members of the group will be there for the individual when they are in need, just as the individual is available to others in the group. The key here appeared to be the presence of an exemplar in the group who demonstrated what deep caring looks like, and then others ended up modeling the same care.

## SERVICE GROUPS

Reciprocity provides the security of believing that the cost of one's efforts in terms of time and money are worth it because they make a difference.[15] Vertical reciprocity ascertains that God is ultimately providing rewards and punishments through cooperation or non-cooperation.[16] Service projects provide this experience to baby boomers in which they are often investing in situations or people who will never be in a place to "return the favor." The opportunity to provide service with religious motivation encouraged many baby boomers to desire to belong.

## STORYTELLING

Baby boomers are grappling with meaning-making as they enter into the final phase of earthly life. As mature adults look back at the gains and losses of their lifetime (and not just their old age experience), there can be a sense of missed expectations or unrealized dreams. Thus, there is an increasing desire to develop life stories that cultivate meaning of their life history, cope with the experiences that they are facing in the present, and deal with the uncertain time that still lies ahead.[17] The three points of religious belonging offer specific opportunities for storytelling: narrative, sense making, and testimony.

14. Putnam, *Bowling Alone*, 21, 134; Harris, "Ties That Bind and Flourish," 123.
15. Stark and Finke, *Acts of Faith*, 46–52.
16. Harris, "Ties That Bind and Flourish," 123.
17. Ramsey and Blieszner, *Spiritual Resiliency and Aging*, 36.

## Worship Setting

The worship setting links one's story to the timeless narrative of Scripture. This narrative prevents simply sharing one's own stories for personal therapy. Baby boomers expressed that they did not want a "dumbed down" Bible story to make it accessible or attractive to culture. Rather than trying to translate the biblical story into a contemporary, more "acceptable" narrative the desire is to be initiated into the original narrative.[18] Numerous baby boomers emphasized the importance of their pastor explaining biblical and historical context so they could truly grasp what the Scriptural narrative was about. The intersection of ritual and narrative creates "a eucharistic community that replays the narrative in deed."[19]

## Small Groups

Belonging in small groups is where "I know I have a place in the community not only as I hear and accept its stories but as it hears and makes room for mine."[20] Yet, we need to consider the challenges that people face as they age and are called on to share their story. Small groups as safe places are critical for storytelling–where stories can still have loose ends. With thick trust and issue-based themes, small group members are encouraged to process their unresolved stories in community. The express goal in this setting is not providing winning advice but a context to practice one's story. There is civility in conversation that "trades more on friendly curiosity—a kind of relaxed diplomacy—than on confrontation."[21]

Small groups done well offer a context for sense making of one's life story—which is a great fit with the aging process. As people move beyond midlife, the amount of time they invest in telling stories seems to increase. Even while listening to the same story over and over again, listeners artfully seek ways to ask questions that show interest and invite the storyteller to reflect more deeply on how their life story intersects with God's narrative. There is listening which is curious and supportive without being patronizing and formulaic.[22]

18. Smith, *Who's Afraid of Postmodernism?*, 77.

19. Smith, *Who's Afraid of Postmodernism?*, 77.

20. Taylor, *Tell Me a Story*, 120.

21. Koukl, *Tactics*, 20.

22. Ramsey and Blieszner, *Spiritual Resiliency and Aging*, 147. Story offers a hopeful

## SERVICE GROUPS

While small groups offer a place for sense making through organic, is-sue-based storytelling, service groups offer a setting for more systematic presentations of one's faith story. Many baby boomers suggested that the composition of their own story offered spiritual growth—even more than hearing the stories of others. Once again, a safe place is required for people to share their testimony of how God has been and is at work in their lives.

One compelling method used by a participating denomination in-volves creating faith story videos of older adults. As a service project, these older adults told their faith story with a particular audience in mind—gen-erally family and friends. The video was then edited to capture key elements and made available. The storyteller did not have "stage fright" with a live audience and was able to process their story out loud. Many participants suggested that they became involved in the project because they wanted grandchildren to know about religion, but they themselves ended up grow-ing in their personal faith as they connected the dots of their story. One specific growth area mentioned was the need to define Christian "glow words" that have been used across a lifetime without consideration of the actual definition.

## RELATIONSHIPS

Intentionality in relationships matters. Default relationships that form through the worship setting, small groups, and service groups are insuf-ficient without focused attention. Key relationships to attend to include linking, bonding, and bridging.

## WORSHIP SETTING (LINKING)

The worship setting provides the religious marker of a linking relationship with God. Worshippers share an expectation of a vertical relationship—that they will be linked to God through authentic interaction. Linking refers to the deepening connections that people find with clergy, and ultimately with

---

place to engage baby boomers on their spiritual journey. A helpful reminder for this journey is that the "moment of conversion" of Paul on the road to Damascus is not the only biblical paradigm of conversion. The "gradual conversion" on the road to Emmaus in Luke 24 offers another biblical paradigm. Finney, *Recovering the Past*, 40–41.

God Himself.[23] The "upward" relational orientation toward God is critical in order to maintain a clear delineation between a church and a non-church social group that offers support through life transitions. The worship setting provides overt cues through ritual and spoken word about religious linking. For baby boomers, it is important that the "glow words" that they learned about Jesus in their youth are defined and clearly applied so that true emotion and feeling follow.

## SMALL GROUPS (BONDING)

Small groups are especially well-suited to offer bonding relationships where baby boomers have a felt need to discover emotional support. Bonding relationships are those that are between people who are close—family, well-acquainted neighbors, and friends.[24] These bonding relationships are inward looking and focus on those within the existing group. It is the superglue that holds a group together and provides solidarity and a clear path of interpersonal reciprocity.[25] These relationships are usually between people who are like us, hold similar interests, enjoy talking about the same things, and are "normal" in our eyes.

Bonding relationships are the deep and abiding trust-filled relationships that develop amongst members.[26] Small groups tend to have this sort of tight-knit relationship pattern in which the social networks are dense and lead to greater commitment of people in the group.[27] This is a winsome characteristic for adults who are seeking social support amidst life transitions. Not only is there greater commitment in small groups with high bonding relationships, but there is also more shaping and molding of member behavior.[28] There is a greater role for sanctions in a place in which people are deeply connected and can hold one another accountable. Bonding relationships were often mentioned as positive influencers of religiosity.

23. Maselko et al., "Religious Social Capital," 760–61. See also Coleman, "Religious Social Capital."

24. Woolcock, "Place of Social Capital," 71–72.

25. Putnam, *Bowling Alone*, 22–23.

26. Maselko et al., "Religious Social Capital," 760–61. See also Coleman, "Religious Social Capital."

27. Stark and Finke, *Acts of Faith*, 160.

28. Stark and Finke, *Acts of Faith*, 160.

Yet, bonding relationships can be toxic without intentionality. Since deeply bonded relationships put one's life stories on a public stage with close friends and family, there is the potential of an elevated role of shame that gives bonded relationships tremendous influence over behavior.[29] This is a powerful element of covenant living—there are fewer secrets kept from one another. However, if everyone "knows my business" in a small group that includes my family and neighbors, then there might be a heavy burden of shame to bear.

Beyond the issue of shame within bonding relationships, there is also the dark side of bonding where certain groups and their ideas are marginalized as a byproduct of deep in-group bonding relationships.[30] If there are existing small groups (i.e. family or natives) who go out to eat together, who talk about church business together, who go to the same family functions— then it can be very hard for a reengaging adult to break into the inner circle. The tighter the bonding relationships are amongst people within the small groups, the harder it is to enter the group. New adults can be welcomed into the church as family—but remain a second cousin. The opportunity for porous group boundaries comes through service groups.

## SERVICE GROUPS (BRIDGING)

The open, organic nature of service groups provides for bridging relationships—places of engagement with people from different groups, where connections deepen between people who are simply different from one another.[31] In many ways, bridging is the "sociological WD-40" that frees things up to allow for relational connections with people outside one's own social network.[32]

This is quite a bit different than bonding relationships where the ties are strong. The "strength of a tie is a . . . combination of the amount of time, emotional intensity, the intimacy (mutual confiding), and the reciprocal services which characterize the tie."[33] As we observed with weak trust, there is significance with weak ties. The end goal is to avoid having every

29. Roesch-McNally et al., "Soil as Social- Ecological Feedback," 158.

30. Putnam, *Bowling Alone*, 23.

31. Maselko et al., "Religious Social Capital," 760–61. See also Coleman, "Religious Social Capital"; Beyerlein and Hipp, "Social Capital," 996.

32. Putnam, *Bowling Alone*, 23.

33. Granovetter, "Strength of Weak Ties," 1361.

relationship end with strong ties. For one thing, that would deepen the in-group versus out-group divide. A group is actually more cohesive when there are weak ties present. When we exclusively maintain the strong ties of bonding relationship, people operate within their own group, and do not interact well with others.[34] Weak ties provide the opportunity to bridge between people of various small groups and get them communicating, even if it is not at the deepest of levels.[35]

In addition, people are limited by the number of strong ties that they can have—there are only so many close friends one can maintain. More people can be connected through weak ties than if we only relate to people through strong ties.[36] Service groups offer the possibility of bridging relationships with weak ties, allowing baby boomers returning to faith a porous boundary to cross into belonging.

It is important to note that bonding and bridging relationships are not a binary choice.[37] In fact, high-bonding and high-bridging is a possibility that can be captured within churches.[38] In general, though, evangelical churches have tended to focus on bonding relationships to the detriment of bridging relationships.[39] The churches effectively reaching early old age adults have found an approach that offers bonding relationships within small groups, bridging relationships through service groups, and linking relationships in the worship setting. While this is not meant to be a strict categorization, the general application of proxemic size to nature of the relationship is helpful.

34. Granovetter, "Strength of Weak Ties," 1374.

35. Granovetter, "Strength of Weak Ties," 1376.

36. Granovetter, "Strength of Weak Ties," 1369.

37. Putnam, *Bowling Alone*, 23. Putnam does offer a compelling distinction in function: "bridging and bonding social capital are good for different things. Strong ties with intimate friends may ensure chicken soup when you're sick, but weak ties with distant acquaintances are more likely to produce leads for a new job. From a collective point of view the scope of the social capital we need depends on the scale of the problems we face. . . . In short, for our biggest collective problems we need precisely the sort of bridging social capital that is toughest to create" (*Bowling Alone*, 363).

38. Curry, "Social Capital and Societal Vision," 150.

39. Beyerlein and Hipp, "Social Capital," 1006.

# SECTION 3

CHAPTER 12

# Know the Right Fight

## KNOW THE RIGHT FIGHT

W E have examined how the story of the Mann Gulch wildfire calls us to drop our tools (and maybe pick up others). The story also reminded us of the clarity we need to have when communicating. Third, we learn that this was a fight that should never have been taken on.

It was not until 1978 that the U.S. Forest Service changed their policy that all wildfires should be suppressed as quickly as possible. This is despite the fact that scientists in the 1880s had already outlined the importance of wildfires in forest life cycles.[1] The Mann Gulch Fire was not threatening human life nor significant personal property—yet lives were put in danger to immediately fight it. If we only focus on what we can learn about dropping our tools or communication, we have missed a key lesson of the story. With modern understanding of needing to let wildfires burn as a natural lifecycle, "the battle in Mann Gulch seems worse than pointless" where we engage "in a war that, as we now know, we lose even when we win."[2]

## CO-VOCATIONAL

The first battle that we are going to address is a quiet undertow that erodes many rural ministries. The battle that we fight circles around our time— how do we maximize our ministry time when the needs are so great? How do we maintain a healthy balance? For many in rural ministry, how does

1. Grant, *Think Again*, 11.
2. Schulz, "Story That Tore Through the Trees."

that work when we are bi-vocational? This leads me to one my most unfavorite questions.

"Are you full-time or are you bi-vocational?" That question has always unearthed some of my well-hidden insecurities. In essence, what I hear being asked is, "Are you a real pastor or are you a third-class minister?" My insecurities may be rooted in the fact that the majority of my ministry years have been as a bi-vocational pastor in small, rural churches. Even setting my personal issues aside though, I find this question unhelpful as an icebreaker at gatherings. The next question is no better, "What is your worship service attendance?" Apparently, our ministry only matters with a given critical mass of people gathered.

I would much rather focus on what unites us as pastors – we are all co-vocational. We do not live compartmentalized lives in which some work is for God and some work is simply secular work. We all undertake a wide variety of work during our week—and all of it is for God. All of our work is linked together as Kingdom service (co-vocational), it is not a competition amongst the different types of work that we have compartmentalized our lives into (bi-vocational).

Don't get me wrong, there are differences between pastorates that are compensated to meet all of a pastor family's living expenses and those that do not. What I think is unhealthy is that we somehow conflate compensation into the idea that some pastors "work full-time" and other pastors "work part-time." We all work full-time.

All rural pastors and active church members are co-vocational. We are only in a healthy place if we recognize that our work calling is not a sacred versus secular calling. God calls us holistically. Last I checked, all of us need to do unpaid work: laundry, dishes, yard work, fixing the broken vehicle, driving the broken vehicle to a garage after we broke it more while "fixing" it, helping the neighbor, caring for our children and loved ones, shopping, cleaning—I think you get the picture here.[3]

All of our co-vocational work is in service to God—but it means that we need to be honest about difficult life experiences. Over the last few years, pastors and church members have faced an increasing number of challenges and struggles from all directions in life, not just the "ministry compartment." In many ways, we have been facing a wildfire, and we have lessons to learn.

3. For further treatment of applying theology of work to life see: Peabody, *God Loves Your Work*. Keller, *Every Good Endeavor*.

A couple of introspective questions are worthwhile here as we think about our own personal health for the months of ministry ahead. What are co-vocational elements of my ministry that I tend to overlook? What is ministry service that I am currently doing "under the radar" that still exacts an emotional and spiritual toll? What joys am I missing by not observing my co-vocational work? Finally, how does my congregation affirm or miss my co-vocational ministry or the co-vocational ministry of my pastor? Am I communicating the nature of my calling well?

As rural ministry practitioners in this season, we are called into a posture of learning. One key lesson from the story of Mann Gulch is that the Smokejumper's reputation as fire experts prevented them from seeing what they did not know about a wildfire "blowup" that was taking place.[4] This is not a season for rural experts as much as ministry practitioners with a posture of learning who are focused on the well-being of the crew, not just putting out the fire. We have more learning to do as we consider some of the other fights that we are entangled in as rural ministry partners.

Focus on the well-being of the crew begins with assessing the health of rural ministry leaders—such as honestly looking at our own co-vocational use of time and celebrating the co-vocational ministry of those around us. We also need to know how to define our rural crew. What is, after all, our rural community? Defining that community, and whether or not it is "really rural," often involves a fight. One that does not need to be fought.

4. Maclean, *Young Men and Fire*, 19, 33.

# CHAPTER 13

# Stop Whining

*Ruralization of America*

A FIGHT we need to put an end to is talking about rural ministry as "not suburban or urban." While there are elements of truth to "rural is not" descriptions, we end up describing rural ministry in the negative. Rather than contrasting rural ministry ad nauseum, we have the opportunity to describe rural ministry in a winsome way.

The ruralization of America is underway, and it has significant impact on our approach to ministry as rural practitioners. The demographics often touted present the picture of a shrinking rural population and rural space in America but overlooks the countervailing rural cultural influence. Likewise, we often describe our unique rural ministry approach as what is not urban or suburban, without proactively stating what rural ministry is. We should change our tune.

We know the general melody played about urbanization of the United States, where there has been a tremendous shift of population to urban areas over the years. Increasingly, we are also hearing about the ubiquitous impact of urbanism, the growing influence of urban life through sociocultural and symbolic influences.[1] The conclusion drawn is that there has been a "massification of rural society" through globalization, and the urban dominated world leads to a less distinct boundary around rural.[2]

---

1. Lichter and Brown, "Rural America in an Urban Society," 565–92; Brown and Schafft. *Rural People and Communities*, 16–17.

2. Lichter and Brown, "Rural America in an Urban Society," 567.

However, what if the increasing interface (rather than boundary) between rural and urban not only reflects urbanism, but also a rising ruralization? "If the whole world is urbanizing, it *must* also be ruralizing."[3] The interface of rural and urban interaction, the many gray spaces of where urban and rural meet, is not a unidimensional power play of urban on rural. Rural is simultaneously engaging in a countervailing influence.

## SEEING THE INFLUENCE OF RURAL

Think about how we see the countervailing influence of ruralization of the urban. Urban and suburban development is often designed with green space and amenities to give it a rural flavor. We generally talk about the triumph of urban and suburban areas over the rural due to sprawl and expansion. But the nature of that expansion has reflected a ruralization of our culture. The sprawl and the decentralization of many urban areas is an effort to make it look less urban and to feel more rural. The urban has experienced a change in identity as it is less of a core and becomes more sprawling, reflective of rural more than traditional metropolis.[4]

There are many examples of how even ruralism is impacting America. American personalities often seek out ways to look or convey a rural vibe. A compelling example is connected to Cowboy and Western movies portraying American values. A specific example is George W. Bush purchasing a rural ranch before his run for president as a means to connect to the common person.[5]

I am not completely detached from reality—rural is certainly being influenced by urbanization and urbanism. At the same time, we do a disservice if we do not recognize that there is a countervailing ruralization and ruralism being felt in America. In regard to rural ministry, a key cultural phenomenon to respond to is the hunger for place.

3. Krause, "Ruralization of the World," 233–48.

4. Cloke, "Conceptualizing Rurality," 18–28; Woods, *Conceptualizing Rural Areas*.

5. Lichter and Brown, "Rural America in an Urban Society," 570.

## BELONGING AND PLACELESSNESS

There has been a tremendous amount of ink invested in the importance of providing people with a sense of belonging.[6] In fact, we have already described that need in this book! So, let's continue assuming that belonging is a great opportunity for the church. A specific application of belonging involves our hunger for place.

The 1970s, marked an increasing focus on the differentiation of space and place. Space refers to the spatial proximity of something, or the arrangement of things within certain boundaries. Place, on the other hand, is linked to meaning given by nature and culture. Hence, place defines space, "giving it a geometric personality."[7] A neighborhood is first a blurry space, through experience it can become a place.[8]

Architects largely discounted the idea of place and focused on maximizing space rather than shaping experience. Meanwhile, a rising tide of voices were pointing out that building spaces rather than places was leading to increasing placelessness, "the weakening of distinct and diverse experiences and identities of places . . . from a deep association with places to rootlessness, a shift that, once recognized and clarified, may be judged undesirable and possibly countered."[9]

By the 1990s, there was a rising sentiment that we had gotten zoning rules wrong. The sprawling post-World War II suburban expansion was designed to be less like the city core and more like a quasi-rural experience, enabled by the rise of the automobile. But something was missing. The creation of a rural-like experience with the nearby amenities and work of the city ended up to be a counterfeit. We had lost the sense of place that a city core or rural area offered through social interactions that came with "place." The suburbs were a space, intended to give an individual or a single family the ideal life. Without the sense of community offered by a city core or traditional rural towns, a sense of placelessness permeated the experience.[10]

---

6. Myers, *Search to Belong*; Myers, *Organic Community*; Moon and Simon, *Effective Intercultural Evangelism*.

7. Tuan, *Space and Place*, 17.

8. Tuan, *Space and Place*, 17.

9. Relph, *Place and Placelessness*, 6.

10. Kunstler, *Geography of Nowhere*.

## HUNGER FOR PLACE

Part of the ruralization of America can be seen in the nostalgic hunger for place. There are plenty of examples of previous suburban dwellers who have become captivated by the rural life and transitioned to where they find a sense of place, a connection with home. A dramatic example of this transition is by Christopher Ingraham who famously wrote a story in the *Washington Post* about the "worst place to live in rural America," and then ended up moving he and his family to that small, rural town in Minnesota.[11]

The idea of place is not simply waxing eloquently about nostalgic themes though, there is money involved. And, when there is money to be made, we can learn all sorts of interesting things—such as what people are willing to pay for. In a fascinating study of Cracker Barrel restaurants, the authors found that Cracker Barrel restaurants:

> . . . cultivate a strong sense of place through careful theming, generating a distinct sense of rural America and nostalgia for home. At the same time, the uniformity of Cracker Barrel speaks to the notion of placelessness, the eradiation of unique local features and homogenization of experience. Cracker Barrel is thus simultaneously placeless and place*full*."[12]

Notice, Cracker Barrel restaurants are carving out their niche by trying to look rural, often in very non-rural settings. The specific approach the restaurants are using is to develop a sense of place that connects with what people long for—either from nostalgic memories or the rural idyll that they have seen popularized on screen or in print. What is amazing, is that they are doing this through developing a counterfeit sense of place. They use memorabilia and decorations that symbolically link people with a nostalgic sense of rural place, without actually creating it.

People are hungry enough for rural place that they will accept a franchised version of it. In contrast, the rural church can provide the real thing—belonging in a true sense of place. We have the opportunity to unapologetically meet a need for place.

11. Ingraham, *If You Lived Here.*
12. Gregory and Finlayson, "Paradox of Cracker Barrel," 258.

## RURAL MINISTRY IN PLACE

> It's true that people need places to live, and I don't begrudge any-
> one the dream of owning a pretty house for their kids to grow up
> in—but I believe we need more than just houses. We need *homes*,
> and a home is more than just the four walls where we eat and sleep
> and watch Netflix. It's a place that shapes and gives meaning to our
> lives. We need Places with a capital P, places that honor the com-
> munity's history, the sacredness of creation, and our basic human
> need for beauty and nature.[13]

If we listen well to this quote, we hear the impact of the ruralization of
America. There is a search for Place—that connects with very rural tenets.
Community history. Connection with creation. Link to beauty and nature.

Our usual ministry posture is one of defensiveness as rural ministry
practitioners. Since we are a shrinking minority, as conventional wisdom
goes, we need to carve out what continues to make our ministry call different. At the same time, we should be proactive in our ministry posture.
There is a ruralization of America underway that also opens the door for
ministry approaches that are more than defensive. We have an increasing
opportunity to connect with people in very real ways.

The rural church has the opportunity to provide a "capital P" Place
for people to belong. The rural church has the opportunity to partner with
her community in ways that fosters a resurgence of place in the town and
village. The rural church also has the opportunity to see that there are not
distinct boundaries around who is "rural enough" to respond to rural ministry. The ruralization of America creates a hunger for what rural ministry
offers.

The key is to recognize that Place is not something that just happens.
It requires intentional attention and fostering. We have that opportunity
in rural ministry. Not as a defensive tactic because no one understands us,
but as a proactive opportunity that we are the most equipped to undertake.
Let's steward this gift well.

13. Peterson, *God of the Garden*, 160.

## CHAPTER 14

# Rural Ministry Assessment

## PART 1: THE PLACE AND THE PEOPLE

W HEN people ask me to talk about my family, I invariably talk about *where* we live, but I focus most on *who* we are. Do we do the same when we are asked to describe our rural ministry? While we should know the uniqueness of our rural context and how it shapes ministry, the rurality of the people themselves is the necessary key to contextualized ministry. Rather than merely describing the rural place by thresholds such as low population and sparse population density, we need to be able describe the subculture of the people. In order to better reach the people of our rural communities, we need to know how to best observe and learn from the people.

Here is one fight we need to stop: arguments over the exact boundaries of what "really rural" entails. That is a fight based more on anecdotal assumptions rooted in our (my) location specific experiences. It is when we set that fight aside that we can better delve into the data that is truly helpful to learn alongside our neighbors and communities.

### RURALITY[1] SUBCULTURE THEORY

There has been considerable debate about what "place" differences exist between rural and urban/suburban contexts that can be measured, and if

1. Rural refers to the Latin noun, *rus*, which focuses on the place as an open area, specifically outside of cities. Rurality was most likely built off the French word ruralite, referring to the "condition of being rural." Woods, *Rural*, 4.

those differences still exist in the 21st century.[2] Even more, there is disagreement over the nature of the spatial boundary that theoretically exists between rural and urban—whether that liminal space is a divide or place of integration.[3] Rather than getting bogged down by establishing whose context is really rural based on spatial boundaries, subculture theory provides a framework upon which to build.[4] Subculture Theory moves us back to focusing on people, not just place. That seems like the right place to start when we are talking about ministry.

Subcultures are not purely bounded, exclusive groups, yet there are some important affinities in place.[5] A subculture consists of people who: mutually possess or practice a distinctive trait, hold a unique set of values in common, share a common way of life as expressed through behavior and artifacts, are identified as a group, and/or interact with one another within their group more than those outside the group.[6] This definition has us well on the way to observing how our local rural community is unique as a subculture. Let's look at the delineations of note as we think about our rural neighbors. When we recognize what makes our rural community distinct, we also better understand how to connect with it.

2. As urbanization and industrialization firmly took root in the late 19th and early 20th centuries, social science titans such as Durkheim (Durkheim, *Rules of Sociological Method*) and Wirth (Wirth, "Urbanism as a Way of Life," 1–24) took note of the increasingly perceived differences between rural and urban. Shucksmith and Brown, "Framing Rural Studies," 2; Brown and Schafft, *Rural People and Communities*, 3; Thomas et al., "Response Styles," 99. These perceived differences became more systematized as theory was increasingly augmented by empirical study as well as the implementation of government policy and programs based on rural and urban distinctions. Panelli, "Rural Society," 64.

3. Lichter and Brown, "Rural America in an Urban Society," 565–92; Lichter and Ziliak, "Rural-Urban Interface," 6–25; Lichter et al., "Rural-Urban Interface," 1–14.

4. Thomas et al., "Response Styles," 99–100, 102.

5. Fine and Kleinman, "Rethinking Subculture," 8.

6. Fischer, "Subcultural Theory of Urbanism," 544; Gelder, "Field of Subcultural Studies," 1; Fine and Kleinman, 18.

## Labels

First, subcultures are self-ascribed, or their label is placed by people from outside the group.[7] This identification can come because the group is seen as non-normative or as a marginalized group.[8]

I think that we can all point to recent conversations in which rural people were described as economically left behind or facing unique challenges social challenges. That is a recipe for a subculture. In addition, since there is discussion about *how* distinctive rural is, there is a clear identity of this group from a self-identified standpoint, as well as academic and popular discussion of unique rural voting patterns, socio-economic characteristics, and cultural artifacts. The question is about "how much" identity rather than "if" there is a rural identity.

The label on our local community makes a difference. Whether the rural label is given by the local population itself or is applied by people outside the community, it creates a socially constructed reality. We are shaped by the expectation of our identity. A simple question to ask here is: *what rural label does my community wear?* Labels such as farming town, economically depressed, retirement community, summer get-away, college town, bedroom community, etc. will give a good idea of the identity that will be shaping people.

## Centrality and Saliency

A second delineation of interest is that a subculture is one of many identifications. Two key items to notice within subculture identification are centrality and saliency. Centrality refers to the level of commitment that an individual has to a given subculture. Saliency refers to the frequency with which the subculture is referenced.[9] Simply put, centrality is how important the rural identification is to their identity, and saliency is how much they talk about it.

While there is an ubiquitous rural subculture given self-identification and externally-ascribed identity through media and statistical reporting, both centrality and saliency vary significantly depending on the unique

7. Brewer and Gardner, "Who Is This 'We'?," 83; Gelder, "Field of Subcultural Studies," 1.

8. Williams, *Subculture Theory*, 1.

9. Fine and Kleinman, "Rethinking Subculture," 13.

rural context. Centrality and saliency are key to understanding the uniqueness of the rurality of the people in our community. A question to ask here is: *what is my first impression of the centrality and saliency of rural identity in my community?* We need to look beyond what the identity is and see how much it influences.

## Group Consciousness

A third delineation to note is that a subculture can be "expected to develop in any category of the population of a society when its members interact with each other more than they interact with persons in other categories."[10] This provides the framework of a sense of group consciousness that is built through social interactions and networks.[11] Once again, this is another quintessential element of many rural communities.

Our identity is strengthened when there is reinforcement through overlapping relationships. A question to ask here is: *how thick are the overlapping relationships in my community to shape a deeply embedded rural subculture?*

Recognizing the importance that subculture theory ascribes to labels, centrality and saliency, as well as group consciousness, will help assess whether or not the rurality of my neighbors impacts my ministry approach. If labels are limited, centrality and saliency comes from competing non-rural identities, or there is a lack of group consciousness, maybe I should rethink how "rural" my ministry approach should be. Reflecting on these three questions prepares us for the oft overlooked next step in rural ministry assessment: ground-truthing.

## PART 2: GROUND-TRUTHING

Is there a magical population cut-off between rural and not-rural? Is there a population density that is a light switch change between a rural village and an urban city? Is 44 minutes to the closest Walmart not distant enough to be rural while 46 minutes makes me rural? If the town I have lived in my entire life has seen a population surge over the past 20 years so the place is no longer rural, does that mean that I do not have a rural identity?

10. Rose, "Subculture of the Aging," 123.

11. Rose, "Subculture of the Aging," 126; Fine and Kleinman, "Rethinking Subculture," 18.

With questions like this in mind, I am making the case that we need to qualify statistical thresholds of place by focusing on the people, representing a social constructivist approach to rural assessments.[12] We generally run to a threshold approach for describing a rural place where our ministry is based. We talk about population, population density, the distance from urban areas, the travel time to the closest Walmart or McDonalds. This is good, but we can become fixated on a variety of census-based measurements of place and miss the people.

## Social Constructivist

The thresholds utilized are focused on the place while the social constructivist approach focuses on the "rural idyll"—a perceived contrast to urban culture that may not be measurable in objective means, but is felt by people based on their subjective daily experience.[13] Simply put, demographic thresholds assesses rural as a place while the social constructivist approach assesses rurality of the people. Focusing on people builds on the sense that devising "excessively complicated classifications" to universally describe rural contexts is a miss.[14]

There is a necessary qualifier here though—a purely social constructivist approach to rural could mean that a resident of New York City self-identifies as rural, and therefore is classified as rural regardless of the context.[15] There need to be boundaries, especially since rurality "is too often the subject of sentimental commentary"[16] fueled by a "lack of empirical clarity."[17]

---

12. While the demographic threshold approach has in large part held sway in North America, the social constructivist approach came as something of a critique to the thresholds-based analysis of rural, and became very prominent in the UK during the 1980s and 1990s and subsequently has had an influence on North American perspectives as well (Shucksmith and Brown, "Framing Rural Studies," 2).

13. Bell, "Fruit of Difference," 65–82; Halfacree, "Rural Space," 18–28.

14. Halfacree, "Rethinking Rurality," 304.

15. For the social constructivist attempting to find some middle ground, it is essential to note that "rural as a distinctive type of locality and the rural as a social representation" are complementary. Halfacree, "Locality and Social Representation," 34; Halfacree 2005, 49; Brown and Schafft, *Rural People and Communities*, 5; Cloke, "Conceptualizing Rurality."

16. Hoggart and Buller, *Rural Development*, 1.

17. Halfacree, "Locality and Social Representation," 32–33. One extreme of social

In the end, rural ministry would be best served by examining three key areas: 1) the rural place, 2) ways that the rural area is represented, and 3) the lives of the people living in that rural area.[18] Ground-truthing provides the potential corrective through developing and refining the thresholds of place that are appropriate for given contexts[19] while simultaneously listening to the people themselves.

Ground-truthing = Census Data of the Place + Interviews with the People

## GROUND-TRUTHING

Ground-truthing offers an opportunity to qualify helpful threshold-based measures such as the United States Department of Agriculture Economic Research Service Rural-Urban Continuum Code through case studies to confirm the validity of the assessment. First, ground-truthing uses mixed methods in which spatially-oriented thresholds are used in conjunction with qualitative studies to offer the opportunity for triangulation and better reflecting the true nature of rurality in a given context. Second, it is "research with rural communities and respecting their forms of knowledge" rather than simply a top-down approach by distant researchers. Third, the thresholds and qualitative studies can be developed to best assess a given purpose. In some cases, the ground-truthing might question the results of the thresholds-based analysis, in other cases the qualitative studies might reveal a socially constructed myth about the nature of the people and area.[20] In addition, ground-truthing might provide an opportunity to develop and refine the thresholds themselves that are appropriate for given contexts.[21]

---

construction was to see that the assumptions and imaginations about rural had become so removed from the reality of the place that rural was "deterritorialized"—where we are simply left with "virtual rurality." Cloke, "Conceptualizing Rurality," 22; Shucksmith and Brown, "Framing Rural Studies," 4. This extreme, hardened approach to social constructionism has in large part fallen out of favor since the 1990s. It is, however, important to note the ongoing influence of social constructionism in rural research. Castree and Braun, "Constructing Rural Natures," 161.

18. Halfacree, "Rural Space," 52.

19. Patrick, Statement at ERS Workshop, 117.

20. Shucksmith, Statement at ERS Workshop, 113–14.

21. Patrick, Statement at ERS Workshop, 117.

## Rural Ministry Application

We might live in a rural place, but do we wear our rural identity? We can describe a place as rural, but it misses the ministry importance of rural—namely, how the context influences the people. Assessing the uniqueness of our location is important—knowing what type of rural place we minister in based on population, land use, and remoteness shapes how we can best connect with people in their third places and civic networks. Yet, we have a truncated approach if that is where we stop. Simply put, there is no substitute for getting to know the people.

As we listen to people's stories, we learn more about the place while we start to grasp the rurality of the people. When we listen to stories with intentionality, we begin to hear how influential the rural identity is for people. That has a dramatic impact on rural ministry: just because it is a rural place, the people might not respond to rural ministry approaches because of their primary identities. On the other hand, a place that is not demographically rural may have enclaves of individuals who hold fast to a rural identity and will respond to rural ministry approaches.

Questions to consider: *Am I creating opportunities to listen to my neighbor's stories to discern how rurality influences their interests and learning styles, or do I use the rural nature of a place to assume that people in this neighborhood will respond to generic rural ministry approaches? Am I listening for the unique specificities of my rural community in conversations, or simply assuming that there is a generic rural culture?* We will now work our way through these questions as a means of refining our rurality assessment tools.

## PART 3: WHICH HAT SHOULD I WEAR?

When winter settles in here in Wisconsin, it is the season to break out snug, well fitted hats. The question is, which hat do I select? I could go with a tractor theme, in which I need to choose between the green and yellow hat (of my in-law's farming tradition) versus a red and black themed hat (of my own family's heritage). Then again maybe I should go with a more neutral theme of general workwear. But do I go with my Carhartt or my Duluth Trading hat—which registered trademark do I want to proudly display for my neighbors to see?

## CENTRALITY AND SALIENCY

As we get to know the people in our community, it is important to not just observe what "rurality" they are feeling, but how much they are feeling. As previously mentioned, there is importance to observing the centrality and saliency of a subculture identity. Centrality indicates how much the individual relies on rural as a marker of their identity. We all have plenty of identity markers, but we can only use a limited number as our primary identifiers. Centrality goes beyond examining if the person lives in a rural area, and into how intensely they express the importance of being rural. Is rural a predominant identity marker, or does one's affiliation with a football team, or career type, or socio-economic status serve as a more dominant identity marker? Clearly, discerning what subculture is most dominant would impact ministry approaches.

Saliency reaches into the space of how often a person has the opportunity to reveal or live out their rural identity. Even if a person highly values their rural identity, they may not be in a setting where they are able to talk about it or live like their rural identity matters.

There are differences in centrality and saliency. The following chart provides a review of how central rural identity was portrayed through a series of rural interviews.[22] The first bar indicates the number of participants in each level of rural[23] (less, moderate, and most) who really did not express rural as an important part of their identity. The second column indicates the number of participants in each zone of rural who shared stories that indicated that their rural identity is of some significance to their identity. The final column portrays the number of participants who shared stories that highlighted the significance of their rural identity.

22. The research was with thirty-one rural baby boomers in the Midwestern United States who identified significant spiritual growth over the past ten years, moving from a place of nominal Christian faith to a born-again faith in Jesus Christ. Greene, "U.S. Baby Boomers."

23. This delineation is built from the USDA ERS Rural-Urban Continuum Code, in which zones 7–9 are the most rural, zones 4–6 are moderately rural, while zones 2–3 are actually within metro areas but still have enclaves of rural expressions. For more information, see: United States Department of Agriculture Economic Research Service, "Rural-Urban Continuum Codes."

## Centrality by RUCC Zone Cluster

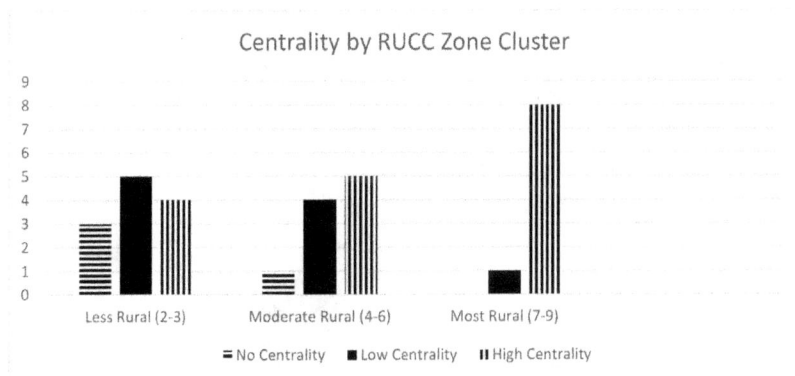

**Rural Identity Centrality by RUCC Zone Cluster**

As indicated by the chart, all zone clusters have people who identify their rurality as a significant part of their identity. The less rural zone cluster (RUCC 2–3) is a blend of centrality—25 percent really do not see their rurality as significant to their identity, 42 percent indicated that rurality influences their identity, while 33 percent shared stories that indicate that rurality is a significant part of their identity. While there is more distribution of centrality than the other zones, it is important to note that the vast majority of these residents still identify as rural even though their zone demographics technically place them beyond the bounds of nonmetro areas. Their area's population or population density is high for rural, or they are not remote from an urban area—yet most identify the importance of their rural identity that continues within their rural enclave.

When it comes to the moderately rural zone cluster (RUCC 4–6), only 10 percent indicated that rurality does not impact their identity, 40 percent shared stories that indicate that their identity is influenced by rurality, and 50 percent shared stories that indicate a significant sense of identity from their rurality. The most rural zone cluster (RUCC 7–9) displays the most centrality of rurality: 0 percent indicate that rurality does not influence their identity, 11 percent shared that rurality matters some to their identity, while 89 percent indicated the significance of rurality on their sense of identity.

While increasing centrality of rural identity with greater rurality is intuitive, it is noteworthy that all zone clusters demonstrate significant identity markers from their context. There is certainly variation based on the RUCC zone cluster, but there is also consistency of a general rural identity influence.

The saliency of rurality follows a similar pattern as with centrality. The stories of the thirty-one participants were coded to observe how often the participants engaged in rural-specific topics.

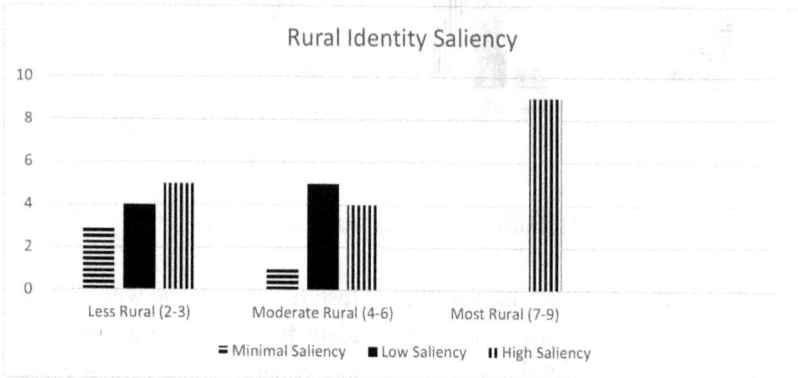

Rural Identity Saliency

Once again, there are clearly different perceptions among participants based on rural zone clusters. Participants in the most rural zone clusters perceive that rurality conversation topics are much more commonplace than the overall experience of those in less rural zones, while those in the moderately rural zone cluster fall in between.

## GROUND-TRUTHING: THE INTERSECTION OF PLACE AND PEOPLE

The less rural the zone cluster (a measure of place), the greater the variation of centrality and saliency of rurality within that cluster. This finding coincides with the concept of the less rural zone cluster being more of a refuge experience, where some places in this cluster serve as a significant refuge from urban influence, while others are mostly integrated into the urban fabric. Ground-truthing is especially important in these settings.

Likewise, even in the moderately rural zones, ground-truthing reveals that there is variation in how central the rural identity is and how salient, or how often people talk about their rural identity. This means that simply applying a rural ministry approach in a moderately rural place may not really be a connection with the people, even though it is representative of the place. If people identify more with their geographic region or with their profession, focusing on rural specific ministry approaches is not necessarily going to connect well. This is especially important given the percentage of the rural population that lives in these moderately rural zones.

Finally, in the most rural zones, centrality and saliency of rural identity were consistently significant. Once again though, this does not mean that a general rural ministry approach is the ticket. The variability of rurality must still be taken into account—trying to establish a Cowboy Church in logging town is a wacky miss.

## What Does it Mean?

We should not stop doing our demographic research of our rural communities. Context matters. Yet, we are on course for a miss if we do not qualify that research with interviewing the people. Before we develop a rural ministry approach for our community, we simply need to get to know people and listen to their stories. That means listening for community rituals—what are the seasonal gatherings and parades that celebrate something unique? What is the industry that defines the area (from a socially constructed viewpoint of the people, not just the dollars and cents in the census data)? What do people say is the biggest challenge for their community?

With these questions though, we need to be sure we are chasing the right subculture. We need to listen to know the centrality and saliency of the rural subculture or discover that there is another subculture that is a deeper connection for people in our community. Rural provides amazing places, but it might not be the primary subculture of the people. I hope that we listen well as we get to know the people while practicing ground-truthing.

# CHAPTER 15

# Application of Rural Context Data

W E will now a look at specific data generated by my research in the North Central Region of the United States. Rather than saying "this is how rural ministry works," the goal is to provide tools to observe and listen for how rural ministry can best be paired to your context. One essential aspect of rural ministry assessment concerns how rural residents "feel their context."

The "feel" of a context is a subjective description rooted in a person's specific rural experience. On the one hand, there are rural realities that can be quantified. Rural statistics of significance include population, distance, integration, density, and land use. But there are also rural realities that are softer, socially constructed experiences that include community rituals, third spaces, relationships, local history, and rootedness. As we will see, these socially constructed variables focus on people over place, especially upon how people perceive their self-identified moral bearings, social milieu, and cultural distinctives.[1]

After establishing what residents feel, we will turn to how these factors influence religiosity. We will also observe that the rural context significantly shapes experiences of aging, which in turn further impacts religiosity.

We begin our observations of the diversity of what rural residents feel by looking through the lens of the Rural Urban Continuum Code (RUCC). The RUCC is far from perfect, and it is not the only statistical measure of

---

1. These concepts are well documented: Bell, "Fruit of Difference"; Halfacree, E-mail message to author; Halfacree, "Rural Space"; Cloke, "Conceptualizing Rurality"; Woods, *Rural*; Brown and Schafft, *Rural People and Communities*, 5; Shucksmith and Brown, "Framing Rural Studies," 3.

rural. What the RUCC has going for it is that it places rural on a continuum rather than a binary split between rural and urban. Likewise, the RUCC offers data for every county in the United States and is readily available to the rural ministry practitioner. By going to the United States Department of Agriculture Economic Research Service link, one can find the data for their county and compare it to adjacent counties, counties throughout their state, and even counties throughout the nation.

The continuum boils down a number of rural threshold data points into a single scale, which is incredibly helpful in assessing a place. Rather than using a completely arbitrary set of thresholds to assess rural, rural ministry practitioners are able to utilize a tool developed and updated by the USDA.

The RUCC builds primarily from data generated by the Office of Management and Budget, and also uses data from the U.S. Census Bureau. In broad terms, here is how the continuum is designed:

| Code | Description |
| --- | --- |
| Metro counties | |
| 1 | Counties in metro areas of 1 million population or more |
| 2 | Counties in metro areas of 250,000 to 1 million population |
| 3 | Counties in metro areas of fewer than 250,000 population |
| Nonmetro counties | |
| 4 | Urban population of 20,000 or more, adjacent to a metro area |
| 5 | Urban population of 20,000 or more, not adjacent to a metro area |
| 6 | Urban population of 2,500 to 19,999, adjacent to a metro area |
| 7 | Urban population of 2,500 to 19,999, not adjacent to a metro area |
| 8 | Completely rural or less than 2,500 urban population, adjacent to a metro area |
| 9 | Completely rural or less than 2,500 urban population, not adjacent to a metro area |

**Rural-Urban Continuum Codes[2]**

As we can see, the RUCC includes a nine-point continuum, from one to nine, where nine is the most distinctly nonmetro. For the sake of finding patterns, my study has clustered the RUCC zones into three categories: less

2. United States Department of Agriculture, "Rural Urban Continuum Codes"; Cromartie, *Historical Development*, 149.

rural (2–3); moderately rural (4–6); and most rural (7–9). The RUCC, as developed by the United States Department of Agriculture, is based primarily on population of a county as well as the distance from and integration with urban areas.

One item that I hope is helpful in this book is introducing the rural ministry practitioner to the existence of useful tools that can be used efficiently for assessing their place. The RUCC is especially helpful because it takes both population and remoteness into account—two items that shape the nature of the rural community that we are ministering within.

At this point, I encourage to pause your reading of this book and look up your county's code in the RUCC. You can access the data with this link: https://www.ers.usda.gov/data-products/rural-urban-continuum-codes. aspx. This link will deliver you to a page where you can select the most recent RUCC compilation. Once you open the spreadsheet, you will find the data organized by state and county. Simply sort through the alphabetized listing to find your county and take in the data: county population, the Rural Urban Continuum Code for your county, and the accompanying description.

After you take in this information, read through the rest of this chapter using your own county's data, and the data of adjacent counties as tools to consider the rural nature of your community and the rurality of the people. Notice the nuances of the various RUCC zones, and the specificities of certain localities. Hopefully this shines some light on the uniqueness of your own setting and opportunities to learn more from your community.

## FELT EXPERIENCE THROUGH THE RUCC LENS

Now we will begin applying qualitative ground-truthing to the data that the RUCC provides. There are five key thresholds utilized by the RUCC and simultaneously shared by rural residents in their interviews.[3] These five items include population, distance, integration, density, and land use. Here is the beauty of ground-truthing at work: all five of these RUCC thresholds that shape the degree of rurality for a given county are also something that can be felt and qualified through qualitative research.

As we begin to apply this ground-truthing approach, there are some defining features of each of the three RUCC zone clusters that are important

---

3. For this portion of the research, the stories from interviews with 50 rural residents interviewed were utilized.

to note. The most rural (zones 7–9) have a relatively low county population, where the largest urban area within the county is 19,999 people or less. The most rural cluster is also defined by remoteness, in which there is great distance for "shopping trips" to the nearest Walmart. For these residents, there is a sense that a boundary is crossed going from the rural area to an urban center.

The moderately rural RUCC zone cluster (4–6) is not defined by remoteness as much as "rural sufficient." Residents indicate that there are regional hubs within their rural area, so they do not need to go to metro centers routinely. There is a sense that there is enough population to support local services, while there is not the remote feeling as exhibited in the most rural zone cluster. This zone cluster is noted for larger populations and pockets of higher density as the urban areas within each county can be up to 49,999 people.

The least rural RUCC zone cluster (2–3) presents a socially constructed refuge. Based on RUCC thresholds, these zones are within metro areas. The urban areas within each county have a population of 50,000 or more and the county is impacted by a significant urban presence. At the same time, the ground-truthing conducted through qualitative interviews indicates that there are areas within these counties where the population and the density are both low, providing a distinct "feel" of rural, although it is not remote nor rural sufficient as with the other two zone clusters.

All told, we will observe that while there are clear distinctions between these three RUCC zone clusters, there is also unity in a common rurality, a socio-psychological feeling that there is something unique about the human activity and interaction that takes place in rural places. Also, we will see that there are many instances of variation within each zone cluster that are routinely influenced by population density and land use. As we keep these broad principles in mind, we now turn to the findings regarding specific RUCC zone thresholds.

## POPULATION

Population simply refers to how many people live in a given area. While the RUCC is concerned with specific thresholds for urban areas and composite population of metropolitan areas to assess rurality, rural residents tended to identify themselves based on a simple population figure. Population serves as the most proficient short cut to describe someone's rural experience.

## Population as an Identity Marker

Population serves as an identity marker across all of the RUCC zones. People in all zones utilized a local population statistic to explain where they live. Sarah represents many others who use population as a shortcut to explain their context—she describes her hometown as a place of 600 people with classes in the public school, numbering fourteen to twenty students. Population is used as a descriptive tool because population figures are commonly known, and it also allows others to easily compare that population to their own context. But many rural residents are sharing more about their context than the simple description of the number of people.

Many use population as a measurement of the health of the town— namely if the town is growing, shrinking, or holding its own. Pastor Nick (6)[4] gave the feel of his community by citing the population figure of 537 official residents, but then qualified the population as much less than that due to now vacant houses as younger people move out and older residents pass away. The picture of shrinking population was a marker for many who are concerned about the future of their community—which is in contrast to those who highlighted a rising population as an indication of the vitality of their rural community. Pastor Howard (6) and Pastor Ed (6) shared with great exuberance how the population in their communities more than doubled in the summer when people visit the amenity rich area.

Population is also used as a marker of what is changing in the area, such as the increasing diversity in some locations. The rise of Latino populations was a significant theme, especially in agricultural areas. The rise of retirees from "the city" was mentioned by others, especially those near waterfront or amenity rich areas.

## Population as Critical Mass

Population is used as a shortcut beyond description to give a flavor of how a municipality functions. Pastor Philip (9) is representative of many rural residents who used population as a short cut to explain what is and is not offered by a community. In order to describe the different rural experience between his hometown and his current town, he pointed out the critical mass generated by population. He grew up in a town of 3,000 people compared with his current town of 700. His hometown population created

---

4. Numbers provided in parentheses indicate the RUCC zone of the individual.

enough of an economic base for a grocery store—while his current town has very limited supplies provided locally. He also went on to explain population gradations based on school sports: large towns play eleven-person football, his hometown plays nine-person football, while smaller towns go down to six-person. Population is a descriptor of scale and therefore provides an indication of how a community functions.

Regardless of RUCC zone, rural residents primarily used population statistics for their municipality rather than referencing statistics for the region. More accurately, people turned first to the population of their geographic location: townships, villages, cities, and even unincorporated areas, especially if there is a road sign that has the population posted. Some who live "out in the country" referenced the population of the nearest municipality as their rural identifier. County and region offered a secondary qualifying frame to better understand the local community.

One consistent reference to critical mass was the public school district. Regionalized consolidation has impacted a number of the communities. Some expressed pride and relief that their community had held on to their own schools or had been able to maintain an elementary or middle school in the consolidation process. Others bemoaned the loss of their own school and the impact it has had on the sense of community. Critical mass for a community often connected to the school district boundaries.

Pastor Dan (8) pointed out that there are concentric rings of population that are of importance to rural residents. First, a person describes the population of their immediate community. Second, the population of the county might be referenced. Third, the population of nearby areas may be noted. Pastor William (4) is a prime example of using these rings. He described his community as a corn field around the church building with little population, the county as a primarily agricultural landscape with low population (RUCC zone 4) and then the third ring is a rural driving radius of 20 miles where the composite population of cities is over 200,000.

Through the interviews, there was an interesting discrepancy in certain phrases. For instance, "small town" refers to 4,000 people for Tanya (2) while for Lorrie (9) it is 700 people. The population of rural also varied a great deal. Pastor Matt (4) saw his city of 25,000 as part of the rural landscape while Pastor Don (8) saw his city of 2,000 as a part of his rural area. The reference point for population does matter. Pastor Matt (4) and those from less rural zones compare to metropolitan areas, such as the Twin Cities of MN, and assert that they are clearly still rural based on population.

Pastor Don (8) on the other hand sees a number of small municipalities with "a few hundred people" in his county failing due to a lack of critical mass that fosters functioning as a community. Hence, for Pastor Don, his small city is more linked with a historic rural experience than those from smaller municipalities.

Rural residents feel population and also use it as an identifier. When they are referring to population, their glossary of rural words may be similar, but the definitions vary. The variance is increasingly prevalent in distance and integration.

## DISTANCE AND INTEGRATION

Distance and integration serve as descriptors that highlight differences in the rural experience. Distance refers to how much travel is required to attain necessary goods and services. As we will see, this is measured in reference points of medical care, Walmart, and McDonalds. Integration refers to how much back and forth there is between one's rural community and a large urban area. While distance refers to how far away things are, integration is a measure of how often the trip is made, and how much time someone spends in a large urban area. Integration activities include work, routine shopping, and visiting third spaces.

### Distance and Integration as Identity Markers

There was considerable difference between zones in regard to how much significance rural residents placed on distance. Those from the most rural RUCC zone clusters (7–9) discussed distance as something of a badge of honor. All sixteen participants from the most rural zone cluster (7–9) expressed that they were at a moderate or significant distance from necessary services. A common thread was the discussion of how far they traveled for significant shopping trips—the trip that included stocking up on grocery items, buying durable goods, or going to a chain restaurant. Pastor Seth (7) described the rural experience as living thirty minutes away from the nearest McDonalds. Pastor Dan (8) shared that the nearest mall is an hour away. Pastor Philip (9) said that the nearest place to buy significant supplies was sixty miles, but to have options of stores required a metro area that was 1 ½ hours away.

The moderately rural zones (4–6) mentioned distance much less, and when they did, it was a very subdued discussion. Of the seventeen participants in the moderately rural RUCC zone cluster (4–6), seven of the seventeen did not mention distance in their stories while four expressed that they were close to services and six expressed that they were at a moderate distance from services.

These individuals indicated that their regional area provided most of what they needed. In general, these individuals did not talk about traveling long distance for bulk grocery purchases—they had enough options regionally. While some indicated traveling at a distance for durable goods, that was clearly the exception rather than the rule. As Pastor Matt (4) indicated, most of what you need is in the town or city that you live in or live close to. Even Thad (6), who bemoaned the loss of stores and businesses in his own small town suggested that it was at the expense of an expanding nearby town. The physical distance of travel was not the issue for Thad—his concern was the feel of distance–that his own municipality did not have what it once did.

Those from the least rural zone cluster (2–3) discussed the opposite of distance and focused on proximity. None of the seventeen participants from this cluster (2–3) shared that they were at a distance from necessary services. In fact, fourteen shared stories indicating that their proximity to work, shopping, and services was a benefit of where they lived.

Joe (3) represents this group when he talks about how wonderful it is that there are so many amenities close by but without the traffic headaches that come with a metro area. Overall, this group hardly mentioned the need to travel for significant shopping, but some did indicate that the cost was living in a bedroom community. In zones 2 and 3, the county is deemed a metro county, but there are still areas that "feel" rural. Many of these low population pockets have significant rural characteristics but are close enough to the metro area that they do not have significant businesses or stores in their own community. For Harold (3) and Jean (3), their town does not even have a gas station, let alone a grocery store. However, the city of 60,000 located ten miles away offers an abundance of grocery stores and restaurants. Distance is not an issue—but they have limited third spaces within their own community.

One item worth mentioning here is the creation of medical deserts due to distance. Once again, there is significant difference between the three zone clusters. Pastor Seth (7) shares a common theme amongst those in RUCC zones 7–9—outside of emergency care, there are very few medical services provided. It takes thirty minutes to get to a regional hospital and sixty minutes to arrive at a hospital offering more specific care. If there are life threatening issues, the hospital of choice is two hours away. When it comes to mental health, the desert is similarly felt—there are very few options within two hours. The need is felt strongly enough that a group of pastors, including Pastor Seth, are now taking Biblical Counseling classes to be able to offer mental health services locally.

The moderately rural zone cluster (4–6) residents indicated that there are decent regional opportunities for health care and mental health. If there is a specialized procedure required, a transfer to greater distance is likely, but these are not nearly as commonplace as the most rural zone cluster. On the other hand, the least rural zone cluster (2–3) suggested some transfers to larger metro hospitals, but this was not indicating a desert as much as the opportunity to find the best care option possible.

Study participants in all RUCC zone clusters mentioned the stigma of receiving mental health services. This was especially true for those who have previously lived in more metro areas. Pastor Jim (3) spoke of his experience living in a variety of large metro hubs where people readily sought out mental health services. Not so in the more rural area that he now resides. He finds that the networks of family and friends run deep for support—and also for watching each other's business. There is a reluctance to accept mental health services even if they are locally offered unless the situation is socially constructed as a dire crisis. There is a lack of anonymity in small communities and walking into an office for mental health services will be observed by people who know the individual and their family, and that story, possibly, will be widely shared.

Integration as an identity marker is felt in similar ways as with distance. Integration reflects activities in urban areas that require a lot of time or repetition, leading to opportunities of greater influence. In the least rural zone cluster (2–3), many people said that their place of work and routine shopping is in the urban portion of a metro area. Even a number of third spaces that they referenced were outside of their own community. It was big news for Don (3) and Thomas (3) that there is now a coffee shop in their own community so that their men's Bible Study meets there rather than going to a coffee shop in the metro city five miles away.

The integration of the moderately rural zone cluster (4–6) was much different. Many spoke of the regional employers as very significant for the economic base and also the identity of their communities. Pastor Matt (4) spoke of a large meat packer based in his community that offers plenty of employment options—both entry level and corporate. With significant employers such as this, he sees less influence from nearby metro areas because the small urban areas provide employment, shopping, and services for the area while still maintaining a "small town" feel.

The perception of integration in the most rural zone cluster (7–9) provokes sentiments of reactive resistance. Just as the distance served as a badge of honor, so does resistance to metro influence. Since the distance precluded most people from routine contact with large urban areas, many expressed a sharp line of demarcation between their community and urban. Similar to the moderately rural zone cluster (4–6), these residents highlighted their local employers. Pastor Justin (7) spoke highly of the businesses in his county that provide a great deal of employment: a window manufacturer and the headquarters for the manufacturer of off-road vehicles. His story offered some insights into the differences from Pastor Matt's experience in Zone 4. Pastor Justin said that the corporate headquarters often had difficulties getting people to move to such a rural place for engineering and management jobs. He spoke with amusement about individuals who had accepted a management job and were preparing to move to the town but backed out.

The common thread to the stories is that when the new manager and their spouse reach the halfway point between the nearest metro area and the town, the spouse declares that there is no way that they are going to move to this area. They turn their vehicle around, and never move.

Pastor Justin's story emphasizes the clear dividing line between rural and urban—and that the integration is limited. In fact, the undertone to Pastor Justin's story is that rural is different, and you are expected to assimilate to rural if you move out here. That is very different than Pastor Matt's story in Zone 4. His story is one of a rural difference, but that people are able to move in, adapt, and even contribute to the diversity of the rural area.

## Distance, Integration, and the Feel of Influence

When it comes to distance and integration, there are clear differences in the rural experience expressed by the zone clusters. The most rural zone cluster (7–9) paints a demarcation of the boundary between rural and urban. When one goes on a significant shopping trip or needs medical care, there is a line that is crossed where they enter a different experience. The crossing is usually intermittent and not a significant portion of their week. There is pride in the fact that their area is clearly separated from urban influence—at least compared to less rural areas today.[5]

The moderately rural RUCC zone cluster (4–6) presents a picture of a porous boundary. Similar to the most rural RUCC zones, the focus is on a boundary that is crossed—the difference is that the moderately rural cluster sees the boundary as an easy pass through. While the most rural residents expressed that they need to go to large urban areas at times for certain goods and services, the moderately rural present their boundary crossing as a choice or preference. Likewise, while the most rural residents paint a picture of how hard it is for "city people" to move to their isolated town, the moderately rural do not see a transition to their town as nearly so drastic. Moderately rural zones see difference between rural and urban, but back and forth can take place in healthy ways. Influence takes place both ways—and it is by choice, not forced.

When there is border crossing between rural and large urban, it is by choice, and it does not require a significant investment of time to travel. While the residents of the most rural areas expressed fear of being absorbed by the urban influence if they need to rely too much on those metro hubs, the moderately rural zone cluster residents were more confident that their economic and social base would shield them from undue urban influence even while interacting with metro areas.[6]

5. There is some variation within this most rural cluster based on adjacency to metro counties. While zones seven and nine are not adjacent to metro counties, zone eight is adjacent to a metro county, but is not integrated enough to be considered a part of the metro area. Remember that it only takes a 2 percent commuter flow from the outlying county to central counties for adjacency. The very low threshold for adjacency with RUCC tempers the differences within clusters regarding integration. Based on thresholds, RUCC adjacent counties are between 2 percent and 25 percent commuter flows. While residents from all three zones note the dividing line between rural and urban, the residents in the adjacent counties (zone 8) expressed increasing integration. Pastor Don, Pastor Dan, Ken, and Sylvia all talked about the increasing number of people who are commuting an hour to work in a metro area at least part of the week. Along with the increasing integration, Pastor Don suggested that he has seen an increasing amount of urban influence over the past twenty years as the boundary between rural and urban is crossed more often. While zone eight offers a slightly different experience than zones seven and nine, the end result is the same—there is a distinct urban influence that rural residents are concerned about.

6. All seventeen interviews with rural residents from the moderately rural zone cluster (4–6) were either zone four or zone six—counties that are adjacent to metro

The least rural RUCC zone cluster (2–3) does not see a clearly defined boundary. There is not a significant distance from urban areas and there is also significant integration with those urban areas—to the point of making bedroom communities. There is not a question of influence—it is readily acknowledged that the nearby urban areas shape much of the experience of these rural residents. There is still a sense of a rural identity for many in this group though—their community provides something of a refuge from the strong influence of urban areas. It is difficult to know where the boundary is between rural experience and city experience. Although the distance is minimal and the influence is great, interviewees from this zone cluster indicated that there was still a unique small town feel to their experience.

Overall, the residents of the most rural zone cluster (7–9) indicated that urban influence was in contrast to rural life. The residents of the moderately rural zone cluster (4–6) shared that urban influence is real but is not completely at odds with their rural way of life. Since residents of this zone feel that they are largely self-sufficient within their own zone, they indicate that urban influence is more of a buffet from which they can pick and choose. Residents of the least rural RUCC zone cluster (2–3) paint a picture of ubiquitous urban influence, but that their communities are able to provide a refuge where rural can still be experienced. The rural experience might not be the same as it was in years gone by, but there is still a felt difference of living where they are.

## Density and Land Use

Density and land use are two other rurality thresholds that were expressed by rural residents. This experience did not follow patterns of the RUCC zones—these variables express diversity within each of the zone clusters. Density refers to how many people are living within a given geographic area.[7] The most common assessment of density circled around people per

---

counties. What is significant is that integration was not highlighted as much in these interviews as it was for zone eight, another zone with adjacency. As shared by Pastor Matt (4) and Pastor Howard (4), the self-sufficiency of the moderately rural zone cluster minimizes the fear of unhealthy integration with metro areas. Of interest, there were no RUCC Zone 5 residents represented in this study. Upon further review, there is only one RUCC Zone 5 county in MN and there are none in WI—the two states where the bulk of the interviews were based.

7. While density and land use are not explicitly used in the development of RUCC, they are important factors used to establish urban areas by the Census Bureau and are

square mile. The reference point was usually geographic: a small city, a village, a town, an unincorporated area, or "the country." Land use is a slight variation of density—this includes references to perceived predominant uses: farmland, forest, countryside, or residential. While density refers to how many people live close by, land use provides an idea of what the landscape feels like.

## Density and Land Use as Identity Markers

Density offers a qualification of the population identity marker. Some rural residents provided a "feel" of their rural experience by painting a picture of how many people lived near them. This can be an overall difference between zone clusters but is generally a variation based on where people live within their zone.

Gwen (6) shared the significant change she has experienced between the two communities that have served as her home in the Upper Central Region of the United States. Gwen did not "feel at home" in her first small city because there were so many people close together. When she moved to a nearby village in the same county, she found it much more welcoming where she was not overwhelmed by so many people being in close proximity.

The population change between the two communities is notable: 3,500 in the small city and 560 in the village. While she mentioned the number of people, her focus was how the village offers a context where people are more spread out. Indeed, the population density in the village is just under 170 people per square mile while the city is nearly 1,200 people per square mile. She shudders at the thought of a nearby metro area with a density of nearly 8,000 people per square mile. She just does not see how she can get to know her neighbors in a significant way if there are so many neighbors nearby. Gwen also expressed the link between density and her perception of safety: "I don't want to be, you know, worried about who's gonna break in or what's going to happen or all that."

Harold and Jean (3) live on a farm in a township with a population of just over 2,000 people, which is adjacent to a city of over 60,000 residents. While they allude to the population of their township, the key focus for them is the number of people living around them. Their township population density is less than 100 people per square mile, while the city that the

therefore still incorporated in RUCC variables.

township borders has a density of 1,890 people per square mile. For Harold and Jean, they feel the population of the nearby city because they travel there for work and shopping—but they feel the density of their township even more because it is where their home is located. The low-density context provides a refuge from the nearby population.

Pastor Maurice (7) talks about his city of just over 5,000 people as rural, yet a different experience from the rest of the county. While acknowledging the small population, he notes the different experience based on density of people living close together. The population density of his city is just over 1,100 people per square mile, while the population density of the county is seventeen people per square mile. Over ½ of the county's population resides in this small city. From Pastor Maurice's vantage point, the nearness of people provides opportunities for relationships and ongoing interaction that are more difficult in other portions of the county. At the same time, the place still has a "small town feel" because it is not overwhelming in size.

Land use qualifies the rural experience as well. The farmers in all three RUCC zone clusters spoke of how their rural experience is defined by living "out of town" in the midst of open space and fields. Others, like Cliff (7), described the importance of his rural experience including woods and hunting opportunities just outside his back door. Bonnie (6) spoke of the importance of moving to her lakefront retirement home where there is more open space to enjoy.

Land use seemed to shade people's perception of their community identity as well. People who were not farmers considered their rural area agricultural if a considerable amount of land was in farming. Even if farming was a minor player in the economy of the area, the land use drove perception. Similarly, people who were in an amenity rich area with parks and wildlife areas considered their rural area to be defined by natural resources, whether or not they personally used them. Consistently, visible land use shaped the identity of people whether or not they were directly involved in that use of the land.

## Density, Land Use, and Community

As we have seen, perceptions of density vary within zones because they can be dependent on the specific location that the person lives in. People in the least rural RUCC zone cluster (2–3) might feel more rural because they are located outside of town and city. On the other hand, some people in the most rural RUCC zone cluster (7–9) feel less rural because they are in a small city that has relatively high density. Land use also shapes the rural experience because it shapes a person's identity. Even if the person lives in a higher density area, if the prevalent surrounding land use is agricultural, they are likely to identify as rural, agricultural.

Many rural residents shared that density and land use together shape their experience of community. This was actually a surprise for Rob upon his retirement from farming. He moved from his home on the farm, where the county's population density is seventeen people per square mile, to his retirement home on the lake in a neighboring county where the population density is nine people per square mile. The surprise is that around the lake, he is in a cluster of houses that belies the density of the county. Likewise, the difference in land use offered a new experience. On the farm, he would need to intentionally seek out people to visit unless there was something farm-related going on. In contrast, it is common for people to simply be strolling around the lake or walking along the road. The different land use coupled with more people clustered together has changed his experience of community in which it is now much more organic and not occupationally oriented.

Tanya (2) provides a glimpse of how density and land use can also be something of a life span experience. The fact that Tanya grew up on a dairy farm leads her to identify with her current setting as rural, agricultural. This is despite the fact that she has not been involved in farming for decades and her county no longer maintains a significant farming economy. The land use, however, continues to include farming, and the population density of her part of the county remains relatively low. As a result, she "feels" a certain type of rural that connects with her childhood living on the farm. This nostalgic experience of rural life leads her to share relatively idyllic descriptions of how everyone knows each other in a small town, and how it is such a blessing to raise a family in small town.

Pastor Maurice (7) provides another picture of how density and land use combine to give a sense of community. The land use surrounding his small city is predominantly agricultural, punctuated by the largest dairy farm in his state being nearby. There are a number of other long-term farming families in the countryside that also provide a predominant picture of a farming area. The density of his small city provides something of a hub of community for these farmers to come to—from third spaces to churches. Hence, the farmers in the open space give a sense of community identity (agriculture) while the small city with higher population density offers a place to experience community. The farming rural residents and the city rural residents are experiencing different aspects of rural based on their specific location, yet they are still connected to one another through rural networks shaped by density and land use. They express a common sense of rural community.

## FELT EXPERIENCE THROUGH SOCIAL CONSTRUCTION

As we have already seen, RUCC zone thresholds are enmeshed with the social construction of the rural experience. Population drives critical mass, which shapes the economic and social opportunities of a given place. Distance and integration shape the experience of influence—both the perceived amount of urban influence as well as the interest in resisting that influence. Density and land use shade the community experience that rural residents feel. We now turn to some socially constructed experiences that bloom within this rural context: community rituals, third spaces, relationships, local history, and rootedness. Once again, listen for how these variables are described for studying your own rural community.

### Community Rituals

Community rituals refer to seasonal activities that are a part of the rural experience that were shared as a part of the stories told by the fifty study participants. The seasonal ritual of high school sports was key across all rural zones. Thomas (3), Thad (6), and Ken and Sylvia (8) represent all three zone clusters when they highlight the enthusiasm and community gathering place of "ball games." Thad was able to recall statistics of the glory years of local basketball between 1975 and 1982 when the school was ranked in the state and had a number of undefeated seasons. He was even able to quickly recall the coach's name. The sports season is a big deal for these rural places, especially as this is often the highest level of team sports offered locally.

Opening day of hunting season is a significant identity marker for many. When I interviewed Pastor Justin (7) I worked around his schedule that day since it needed to be after he got back from the woods during "youth hunt weekend." A unique shaper of rural identity for Pastor Seth (7) was the ritual of a local rodeo. The rodeo has been going for eleven years and draws a number of local residents, as well as people from abroad. The baby boomer who organizes this makes sure they have "Cowboy Church" at the June event, but the organizer does not attend a church the rest of the year. The organizer insists on "God and country songs" to be incorporated in the service. At the last rodeo, the message was brought by a man who had survived an attack by a wild animal and attributes his survival to God's direct intervention.

Community rituals also circle around people's life cycles—especially death. A number of rural residents discussed the importance of funerals in their local experience. Pastor David (6) shared that during his pastorate, he has officiated seventy funerals and only twelve weddings. Half of the funerals were for community members who were not a part of the church. Pastor Dan (8) spoke of how everyone "gets religious" around the time of a death and participate in the funeral process. He sees funeral rituals as a significant time of gathering friends and family from the community and linking it with a religious tradition.

Pastor Seth (7) on the other hand spoke of how funerals in his community are often more attuned to the local culture than the theology of the church. He spoke of how people prefer an "American Civil Religion"[8] experience to an orthodox Christian ritual. Pastor Seth suggested that a number of beloved traditions, including the American Legion Chaplain reading from his manual, are an intermingling of the themes of God, family, and country.

Other community rituals that were mentioned circle around remembering historical events. Memorial Day parades and activities or Fourth of July festivities were oft mentioned rituals of significance. Locally significant anniversaries also bring the community together—as well as favorite sons and daughters who now live abroad. Pastor Dan (6) spoke of how his church's 125th Anniversary brought together people connected by nostalgia. People who had been connected as kids, are interested in local history, or wanted to be a part of the celebration flocked to the weekend events. As a follow up to the anniversary, someone who had grown up in the area and moved south years ago donated a thirty-six-foot steeple to provide the final detail for the historic building.

8. As previously referenced, "American Civil Religion" is the phrase developed by Bellah, "Civil Religion in America," 1–21.

While there are a number of community rituals that continue, others are waning, at least in some of the communities. Pastor Don (8) sees the days of "Family Reunions" around Christmas and Mother's Day as something that is fading. Large gatherings of extended families that often focus on the matriarch(s) of the family are not as strong as they once were. A number of participants in the study noted that gatherings now tend to be smaller and the older family members are more likely to be the ones traveling to visit family elsewhere since their schedules are more flexible and their health allows for it.

The shift from large, formal gatherings to more organic, intimate gatherings is reflective of a broader change in community rituals. Many participants noted that fewer people are interested in being involved in formal, routine meetings but are drawn to volunteering for service activities. Paul (2) spoke of the trajectory of the Christian organization for retired individuals in which he is deeply involved. The group started in the 1980s with an average age of sixty-eight, and about 1,800 dues-paying members. The local chapters were focused on a routine business meeting with a speaker and devotion. In Paul's opinion, that formal ritual is no longer appealing, as demonstrated by the fact that his organization is now down to about 700 dues-paying members with an average age of seventy-nine. As Paul sees it, people have "had enough of corporate" and want to engage in informal activities rather than routine, formal rituals.[9]

Of interest, some differences between zones emerged through people's stories. The most rural RUCC zone cluster (7–9) expressed a uniform impact of community rituals—all sixteen participants shared a story of the significance of community rituals in their lives. The next most consistent was the least rural RUCC zone cluster (2–3) in which fifteen of the seventeen shared stories of community rituals impacting their rural experience. Surprisingly, the moderately rural RUCC zone cluster (4–6) residents were the least expressive about these stories. Overall, twelve of the seventeen shared stories about community rituals. Breaking this down even further, all seven pastors in this cluster shared stories about community rituals, but only five of the ten baby boomers shared that community rituals impacted their experience in a significant way.

9. While Paul is speaking of people in general during this interview, he is presenting from the vantage point of a resident in RUCC zone 2.

## Third Spaces

The zone difference among community rituals is also observed in discussions about third spaces. Third spaces refer to where people congregate locally other than their home and work, and there was a great deal of participant emphasis on how this takes place organically. In many ways, there are direct links among stories with Paul's sentiments about the movement toward informal, organic gatherings. But the perceived significance of these gatherings had variation.

The RUCC zone cluster that was most likely to talk about third spaces was the least rural (2–3) in which fifteen of the seventeen noted significant third places for gathering: eleven of the twelve baby boomers and four of the five pastors. The most rural RUCC zone cluster (7–9) was similar, where thirteen of the sixteen shared stories about the impact of third spaces. The difference with this cluster is that baby boomers did not express the same significance as the pastors: six of the nine baby boomers shared about third spaces while all seven pastors did so.

By far, the least likely rural residents to talk about the importance of third places were from the moderately rural RUCC zone cluster (4–6): only eight of the seventeen shared such stories. Even more telling, while five of the seven pastors shared stories about third places, only three of the ten baby boomers did so.

Sylvia (8) shared a common thread of the organic gathering that takes place at third spaces with a grocery store story: "At least us girls know that if we're going to the grocery store, it might take us an hour, because you might stand in line to talk to one friend. And by the time you get to aisle three, there's somebody else."

Pastor Steve (9) notes that the difference of third spaces between rural and suburban is significant and is distinctly felt. He recently took two of his parishioners on a bike riding trip to his suburban hometown. Both men were overwhelmed by the number of restaurant choices in one place—they were used to a handful of local places. For Pastor Steve, this is what makes the rural experience unique: having third spaces is common but having limited third spaces in which organic gatherings take place routinely sets rural apart. In his suburban hometown, it takes intentionality to meet with others at one of the many restaurants. In his rural setting, intentionality is not required because you are likely to run into people routinely at the limited third spaces.

Reading between the lines, Pastor Steve's insights point to the differences between the RUCC zone clusters. Those in the most rural cluster have only a few third spaces to choose from due to the critical mass of the local population. The organic gathering naturally takes place. Likewise, in the least rural cluster, most third spaces are in nearby urban areas, but there are a handful within the community, such as the coffee shop that Don (3) and Thomas (3) were so enthusiastic about. Once again, the limited number of third spaces within the community provide a natural place for spontaneous gathering.

The moderately rural cluster though, has the critical mass to support a number of local venues—apparently enough so that the natural, organic gathering without preplanning is less likely. An interesting sidebar to this is that some churches in this cluster are creating their own third space venues as a niche. Pastor Ed (6) shared how his church bought a local strip club for a third space. As can be expected, this purchase created quite a stir when Associated Press correspondents from the Midwest and East Coast called for details. The church recreated this third space for gatherings, especially for retired people. One of the niches offered is a gymnasium that includes a pickle ball court– something spearheaded by a retired bank president.

While the other RUCC zone clusters are more likely to focus on organic gatherings, a more intentional approach is taken where there are a higher number of third spaces to choose from in the moderately rural cluster (4–6). Pastor Howard (6) went through the significant number of local restaurants, parks, coffee shops, and stores, but concluded by saying that none of these really stand out as unique gathering places. This is very different from Pastor Seth (7) who shared that people do not need the community of a church because they have all the belonging that they need at the "American Pride Café."

Overall, rural residents indicated that community rituals and third spaces are an important part of their rural experience. A recurring theme is zone cluster differences. The most rural (7–9) are shaped by their remote nature in terms of their perceived geographic and cultural distance from urban. The least rural (2–3) are impacted by their sense of being a refuge from the urbanization that is reshaping the context all around them. In a setting of intense interaction with urban, places and rituals that conserve a feeling of rural are treasured. The moderately rural (4–6) exude a sense of rural sufficiency. There is critical mass to support what they need locally, enough so that specific third places or community rituals do not necessarily stand out as shapers of their experience.

## RELATIONSHIPS AND ROOTEDNESS

A sense of unique rural relationships was a common theme across the zone clusters in the interviews. Lorrie (9) shared that "there's a closeness here." Pastor Nick (6) said that in his setting "relationship is everything." Becky (3) provided a picture of the pervasiveness of relationships with her describing how everyone knows everything that you are doing due to overlapping friendships and the grapevine of informal communication.

The reasons shared for this perceived uniqueness of relationships flowed from variables that we have been discussing. The low population provides the opportunity to get to know people well. The density of a small population or the existence of community rituals and third spaces to create density provides a number of other citations of why rural relationships are significant and unique. The focus here is on what has been felt through social construction—not if rural relationships are actually measurably different than urban settings.

There is a clear expectation that relationships matter because of the nature of rural: forty-six of the fifty study participants expressed some sense of unique relationship experience. For many, part of this experience is connected to rootedness to the area: thirty-seven of the fifty participants shared that rootedness to the land or local families is of significant importance in their setting. There was not observable variation between rural zone clusters, the observation of rootedness was consistent.

Ken (8) displayed clear rootedness when he proudly shared that he still lives in the same house that he grew up in. His family's farmhouse has been his primary residence for sixty of his sixty-five years. Tanya (2) highlighted how she raised her family in the same town that her husband grew up in, and that it has been a wonderful experience with long term family and friends surrounding them. She shares that it is "just a small town, you know, normal, nothing extraordinary" but then she goes on to share the significance of close friends and family. She specifically mentions her brothers who are local schoolteachers and another brother who is a police officer. The town might be nothing special, but the "rooted people" are special.

Pastor Jim (3) spoke of the transient ebb and flow of populations in urban contexts, contrasted by the "badge of honor" of deep roots in his current ministry context. He has been surprised to find five generations of the same family who have been in the same church, where three to four generations may even be at worship on the same Sunday. There is a relational goal for people to stay close to family. Pastor Jim further noted that people who say that they have "no family nearby" are usually saying that their family is forty-five minutes away in a larger town or city.

While there was consistency in sharing the uniqueness of rural relationships and the significant influence of rootedness, there was also a clear undertone of a dark side to these rural characteristics. Pastor Jeremy (4) used the analogy of honey to share this picture: it might all be sweet, but if from a local source, the assumption is that that it is full of beneficial goodness, while if the honey is from a distant source, it does not offer the benefits.

Pastor Mark (6) was more direct—he said that the unspoken rule in his town is that if you were not born there, you do not belong. Pastor Jim (3) echoes this sentiment by stating that he will never be considered a member of his rural community. He punctuates this point by saying that his son was four years old when they moved, but his son will never be considered from that town.

Pastor Howard (6) shared a story of how he was looking for a specific, local food. He was directed to talk to someone who had just moved back to the area after living away for thirty years. Pastor Howard found that the person was not an expert on the food, but he was referred to the person because they had a "local last name" and would presumably know about the food since they had been born there.

The implicit concept of belonging based on being "a native" is also conveyed through the informal relationship process that is required to navigate rural tasks. When Pastor Howard (6) and his family moved to their current ministry context, his children became involved in ice hockey. They had never been involved in ice hockey before and did not know that sharpening skates was required. He found out about it when another parent told him that it was mind boggling that Pastor Howard would need to be told that it should be done. The next step was to get the skates sharpened. Pastor Howard was told to find Todd—not an office at the arena or a certain place; he was to find a person. When Pastor Howard found out where Todd does his work, he went there and found that Todd was not there, nor was there a schedule. It is assumed that you know when Todd is available or how to contact him. Once a part of the native network, this is easy to navigate, but at the time Pastor Howard felt like a clear outsider that no one was going to help.

The perception of special relationships and rootedness has the dark side impact of creating "out groups." As expressed by pastors who have moved in, there is a likely experience of being on the outside looking in. In fact, some describe the feeling as "us versus them" between native and non-native, where Pastor Howard (6) was directly told "you're not from around here so you don't understand." The "us versus them" includes native versus transplants, and also full-time versus part-time residents. Pastors of popular rural retirement areas note that people talk about when they became full-time residents as when they actually arrived—it is the marker of when they could begin to be accepted as a local.

The acceptance of "new people" in rural churches tends to be slow as well. Most pastors express that the lay leadership in their church consists exclusively of, or at least includes a vast majority of native, well-established families. The path to the inner circle of relationship networks and organizations appears to be slow and arduous for outsiders. Of interest, many pastors expressed this outsider perception, but the baby boomers who moved later in life consistently shared that the church they attended "felt like family." Some of the difference between pastor and baby boomer perceptions may be that the baby boomers who moved, generally had friends or family living in the area, providing legitimacy to their rootedness. Cliff (7), for instance already had family living in the area that provided a number of relationship connections for him, which ultimately led him to the specific church that he started attending. Also, based on baby boomer stories, the churches that drew them in provided a relational experience that was intentionally designed to be welcoming rather than following the default rural relationship network.

One intentional area that churches provide for belonging is small groups. Curiously enough, some pastors expressed that this works well for those who move in, but not those who are native. Pastor Maurice (7) said that church small groups do not work for natives because they already have their small group time with family and friends. There is no need for a small group to experience life with or to be introduced into relationships because they already have them. Those who move in have a felt need for a small group, but that is not the case for the long-established families.

The existing "family small groups" can have a dark side in the rural subculture as well. Pastor Maurice (7) shared that in his traditionally homogenous area there is "family tribalism." Some families simply do not get along with other families. Some families are resistant to letting others into their relationship network. There is also a fair amount of labeling based on last name—for instance, an assumption of farm productivity based on a last name association.

A number of the rural areas that identify as agricultural made note of the rise in the Latino population due to local employment. While it was noted that integration is slow, most were positive about how accepting the community has been, especially as transience declines—those moving for local employment are now arriving as a family unit and buying a home rather than living in migrant housing. While a picture of increasing inclusion was offered by rural residents of various communities, none of the churches are attempting a multi-ethnic approach. Multiple churches have launched a Spanish-speaking service or have helped launch a church specifically for an ethnic community—but none have worshipping together as a current goal.

In areas where there is not ethnic diversity in the community, there were a few guarded conversations about racism. For the most part, racism was not indicated as a relevant issue for participants, even as many of the interviews were being conducted during a season of great civil unrest in the country surrounding concerns of race and ethnicity. Pastor Seth (7) was one of the few who gave an assessment of ethnicity as a marker of outgroups. He stated that there is widespread denial of racism in his county, but just twenty years ago "the N word" was used within the church. People in his county say that they should be "color blind"—with the underlying sentiment that white rural people are as disadvantaged by economic and social structures as anyone else. In response to Black Lives Matter, Pastor Seth feels that rather than introspection, the knee-jerk response has been defensive signs indicating "All lives matter or blue lives matter."

Pastor Seth goes on to indicate that the racism is from a lack of relationship networks that engage outside one's comfort zone. Most rural people are quick to point out that the KKK rallies in his area are done by "crazy people" and they would never participate in anything like that. This same group also points to "model minority" children from Korea who were adopted by local families and excel in many things that they do. Pastor Seth thinks that as long as "the other" is perceived as similar to someone's ideals, they are accepted. For instance, if a black person was to enter his church, congregants would say, "oh, you're not like them" and welcome them—as long as they assimilated to the local subculture.

Relationships and rootedness provide the context for what many rural residents perceive as a unique blessing of community. There is also the potential shady side of out groups that holds newcomers at arm length, especially those from different socio-economic backgrounds and ethnic heritage. The impact of relationships and rootedness was felt across all RUCC zone clusters, while the impact of local history and amenities is very location specific.

## LOCAL HISTORY AND AMENITIES

All places have history and amenities—but the specifics shape the rural experience a great deal. Pastor Don (8) spoke for many study participants when he said that rural places have a history of independence and pride in identity. How that history of independence has unfolded makes a big difference. Once again, the recurring theme surrounding independence involved whether or not a community has been forced to regionalize, and if so, how much she had to give up. Many provided stories of school district consolidation that led to a diminishment of community identity. Sending children to a regional school means that when they go to a Kindergarten graduation, attend a junior high band concert, or join in the crowd surrounding a high school sports competition, it is no longer linked to their community. The focus of pride and joy are decoupled from their rural place with the loss of hosting a school. On the other hand, those communities that have retained at least some of their schools with regionalization express a very different picture of community engagement.

As already discussed, regionalization of health care systems has created a feeling of winners and losers. This carries over into the local history narrative of wins or losses. Some, such as Pastor Mark (6), paint a very bleak picture of vacant houses, closing businesses, fewer stores, lost opportunities, and financial hardships. Others, such as Pastor Justin (7) provide a stable economic picture in which the community is holding her own and maintaining relatively well. Others, such as Pastor Howard (6) tell of a vibrant, growing economy and population with a bright future ahead. The historical story provides the narrative of why some communities are struggling, others are thriving, and some are holding their own. One key element to the stories involves the amenities that a given area has or does not have.

Two of the small communities that were represented in the study are home to a school in their state university system. This provides a blessing for employment, cultural opportunities, and also a significant reason for younger people to be in the rural area. As Pastor Jeremy (4) observes, this makes his community's rural experience very unique—small town but big university. His community is host to a Walmart, a few hotels, a significant number of bars, and has a number of high wage earners—simply because the university is there. Even those who are not directly employed are "under the shadow of what is going on at the university." The community identity is deeply embedded with that of the university.

Other rural residents mentioned the impact of significant local employers on their local identity. Pastor Matt (4) spoke of a large meat packing plant and corporate headquarters and Pastor Maurice (7) spoke of the largest dairy farm in the state nearby. The impact goes beyond economics into a sense of social fabric of who they are. Pastor Justin (7) spoke of two large employers in his rural area that have a very different feel. The manufacturer of off-road vehicles has gone from a family-owned business to a publicly held business. It is no longer just a "local business" that is "family operated." There are well-told stories of how the company impacted the town when it was still family held. One year when "money was tight and there was not enough for bonuses," one of the owners flew his plane and dropped candy to people's houses for Christmas. Another example is one of the owners going without money to meet the financial obligations to employees. The vehicle manufacturer continues to have an economic impact but has lost the influence on social fabric without the recurring personal stories of local owners. The local manufacturer of construction materials, however, is still family held and continues to shape the pride and identity of the area as it has in the past, at least from the vantage point of Pastor Justin.

The existence of waterfront property has dramatically changed the identity of a number of communities—especially if they are near a good transportation route. A number of the baby boomers interviewed have relocated to waterfront areas after having a second home there for a period of years, leading up to retirement. These are areas that tend to be growing and economically vibrant with many service sector jobs.

Pastor Steve (9) has found that the presence of significant amenities keeps a number of baby boomers local at retirement, and also invites others to settle there. This leads to two very different sets of baby boomers (inter-cohort differences). First, there are those who have deep roots in the area, closely follow local customs and routines, and are "very set in their ways." The second group are people who are retiring to the area, are relocating, and tend to have more openness to new ideas. Pastor Steve finds this second group is more likely to remain seasonal because it is difficult to acclimate to the harsh winters of his northern location.

Local history and amenities point out that rural is flavored by influences that are not purely based on population, density, or distance. There are some other specificities that need to be considered. Pastor Howard (6) observes three strands that shape the context. First, the geography of the place matters. He has found that the northern most reaches of the Midwest are far different than his Texas experience due to geographical differences. Second, rural matters—the size of a place shapes residents' experiences. Third, there are specificities to pay attention to—each local place, such as his small city, all have their own unique features and story that should be noted.

We have now provided a broad survey of the felt experience of rural residents—both pastors and baby boomers. The perspective of pastors has been especially helpful to frame the perceived difference between urban and rural from their perspective since many have experienced both. We now return to baby boomers themselves to see how the felt rural experience shapes change in religiosity.

## DIRECT RURAL CONTEXT INFLUENCE ON RELIGIOSITY

The rural context can shape behavior due to the perception of close relationships and "everyone knowing" what you are doing. There is an accountability to expectations of religious behavior that was expressed by a number of participants. Becky (3) moved out of her small municipality when she started living with her boyfriend because "everybody knew what everybody did . . . I knew it wasn't the right thing to do. I didn't want to embarrass my parents and so I moved out of town to do that." The interplay of rural relational connectedness and shame avoidance was an oft repeated theme in shaping behavior informed by religious values. As presented by Becky, the value she responded to was based on shame not on the guilt of religious sin.

The rural context also has an impact on believing. Especially in the most rural zone cluster (7–9), there are indications of a continued Christendom in which Christian identity and good American citizenship go hand in hand. This creates a level of religious socialization and connectedness to Christianity that is quite different than much of the American populace. The presence of a local Christendom does not necessitate higher rates of church attendance, but a higher identification with Christian morals and values. As noted by Pastor Seth (7), this religious socialization is not necessarily a benefit in moving baby boomers toward orthodox Christian beliefs. The prevalence of American Civil Religion in many rural contexts can be a significant impediment to recognizing the difference between biblical values and American cultural norms.

When it comes to belonging, there are direct influences shaped by the rural context. As we have seen, there is a rural expectation of belonging to community. Rural relationships and the interconnectedness with neighbors were common themes across the RUCC zone clusters. The participants also shared stories that presented a picture of belonging to a church as a rural expectation. The baby boomers did not necessarily attend or even affiliate with a church throughout their lives, but they did express feeling a rural expectation of church affiliation as a part of one's identity.

Belonging to a small group was an often mentioned in-road to reengaging with a church or changing to a different church. However, out groups are a dark side reality to rural relational networks. Out groups develop, unintentionally and at times intentionally, because those who are non-native, ethnically different, or socio-economically separate do not fit the norms of what constitutes a real local. These out groups pose a challenge to belonging but have also provided a unique opportunity for churches that have been successful in pulling baby boomers toward greater religiosity. Small groups are being provided where there are felt needs, especially for those who do not fit the existing community small groups outside of the church. Small groups are also being tailored to complement long-term family and friendship small groups that already exist rather than compete with them.

The impact of small groups and belonging also plays into the nature of belonging based on density. Density impacts whether belonging at a church is more likely to be regional or community based. When the church is in an outlying area, it will most likely be regional, drawing people from a wide variety of places. If a church is located in a densely populated pocket but is surrounded by a vast countryside without appreciable population centers, that church is also likely is to be more regional as it provides critical mass for people to come to. Hence, the experience of belonging to a church can be shaped by the context—from a rural neighborhood church to a rural regional church. While the rural neighborhood church exhibits more of the "small town church" qualities that participants lauded, the rural regional church setting was where most baby boomers reaffiliated. The pathway to belonging in these regional church settings appear to be more open and intentional.

## RURAL AND THE AGING EXPERIENCE

The aging experience is shaped by the lure of rootedness in rural areas—to truly know the people around you and to be known by your neighbors. Rural residents shared this heightened expectation but interspersed were indications of the dark side to relationships and rootedness. While many who have retired or are entering retirement expect their rural context to naturally provide organic opportunities for friendships as work relationships fade, some find that they are on the outside looking in where the rural context is a difficult journey to really engage with their neighbors—at least in a way that meets their expectations.

The result is that the rural context tends to increase baby boomer expectations that supportive relationships will naturally develop, but that same rural context is also likely to generate out-group hurdles. Putting some pieces together: 1) we have observed that the aging process, especially losses, pushes baby boomers toward a desire for belonging; 2) the rural context shapes relationship expectations and experiences of aging baby boomers. The result of high expectations and potentially great disappointments has generated an opportunity for rural churches to pull baby boomers into belonging. Numerous baby boomers shared how their church "feels like family" and meets their expectations, especially during a season of loss. Death or an illness was often the aging catalyst that led to a hunger for relationships that met rural expectations. Since safe places are not necessarily provided organically in the community, the church often times provided that space.

## RUCC ZONE SPECIFICS

We now turn to each rural zone cluster and observe the signature influence of each cluster. While this should not be construed as a strict generalization, the pattern among interviews provides strong support for some defining characteristics.

## Most Rural Zone Cluster (7–9)

The most rural zone cluster was defined by remoteness. The distance between people, both physically and culturally, leads to some unique experiences. The people of this context identified the significance of aging. While there are developmental aging processes that are felt across all zone clusters, the heightened practical needs of residents in the most rural zone cluster are unique. As previously noted, the low population and lacking critical mass for health systems leads to distance from medical services and creates what many describe as a medical desert. The most rural participants in the study clearly expressed the difficulty in arranging for specific medical care—78 percent (seven out of nine) shared stories involving the impact of illness, much higher than in the other zones. There is significant travel involved and when there are lengthy hospital stays there is difficulty in arranging for family and friends to be physically present during the illness. Simply put, a health issue is a big deal logistically in addition to the health concerns. The impact of a health incident is felt deeper in this zone cluster.

There are a few aging-related results due to the desert. The speed of aging may be felt earlier. When specific care requires great sacrifice of time and effort, it comes at a higher cost. Hence, even though the age-related health concern may not be life threatening, the time and effort required to address the concern gives the feel of significant age-related losses. In turn, the age-related health losses tend to be felt earlier, and more of an early old age push in this cluster.

Another RUCC zone cluster influence on aging is the lack of support groups. Given the low population and density, the likelihood of support groups for those going through medical treatments or experiencing death-related grief is low. The lack of support is especially felt in the area of mental health, in which a shortage of local care was a consistent theme. Hence, the desire for belonging due to aging losses is often unmet in this setting, creating opportunities for churches to intentionally provide safe places for baby boomers.

This zone cluster was more likely to identify a distinct boundary between rural and urban and simultaneously express political views that were sharply populist and distrustful of "government" and the "media." This was also the most likely zone cluster where I would receive warnings from the referring pastor to stay away from the topic of politics in the interview. While this sentiment is broadly felt in the current social and political environment, there was a decided difference between this zone cluster and the others in regard to sharpness and expressiveness of sentiments.

These rural residents perceive that they assess current events through a different lens because of their self-identified culture distance from urban. The same is true when it comes to life review of previous normative events that have been lived through. This zone cluster is the most likely to utilize overtly political language when describing past and present events. Likewise, references to qualities of American Civil Religion were most prevalent in this cluster.

## MODERATELY RURAL ZONE CLUSTER (4–6)

The moderately rural zone cluster is unique through its rural sufficiency. The sense that people meet their needs regionally within their rural landscape leads to some unique influences.

There is a strong relationship between generation (cohort) and this moderately rural zone cluster. More specifically, people living in a moderately rural context noted that the changes in religious socialization are being felt more here than in the other two zone clusters. The most rural cluster has minimal cohort differences in religious socialization; the least rural have lived with these differences for a considerable period of time and are more used to the tension.

The moderately rural residents indicated a greater friction between generations. The experience of younger cohorts being less religiously socialized is a phenomenon that is increasingly being felt. This plays out in a number of different ways. For instance, the strain between cohorts regarding worship styles was more pronounced in this setting than in others. There were a greater number of references to "the way we have always done things" by this group of baby boomers. This "way of doing things" is not necessarily tradition: "the way" oftentimes refers to the type of innovation being sought. Baby boomers see choruses and "contemporary music" as innovative because it changed from traditional hymns (twenty to thirty years ago), but that is not what subsequent cohorts are seeing as innovation. Consequently, strain is expressed toward younger cohorts who just "do not get it."

Pastors also spoke of the tension between cohorts in regard to sermon illustrations and use of Scripture. More pastors noted in this context that there needed to be greater intentionality in life application of sermons and Bible studies because baby boomers were different than other cohorts. Likewise, pastors noted that biblical literacy was different between generational cohorts and that impacted expectations of what baby boomers were looking for from church services in comparison to other cohorts. There are certainly exceptions of cross-cohort congeniality in this context, but overall, moderately rural highlighted cohort differences. In reality, the differences may be very similar to other RUCC zone clusters, but the perception is enhanced because of very different socialization patterns and a lack of experience in communicating those differences well.

Going beyond cohort differences, the regional mindset and rural self-sufficiency of these RUCC zones influenced what residents are searching out. Since there are a host of third space options and community rituals to participate in, there is not the routine, organic gathering that is likely in the other two zone clusters. This provides unique pull opportunities for churches. For instance, rather than joining "church small groups" many baby boomers in this zone cluster referred to their entry into church connections as through a nonprofit service project. Sam (4) was involved in sports activities and Arlene (6) was engaged in community service projects that were more of third spaces initiated by churches—but not hosted by churches.

## Least Rural Zone Cluster (2–3)

The less rural zone cluster maintains a rural refuge identity. There are pockets of relatively low population density within the counties of this zone cluster where people experience a rurality that is different than their nearby urban area neighbors.

There is a moderate relationship between the less rural zone cluster and aging—but for very different reasons than with the most rural cluster. While distance drove the unique experience in the most rural, proximity provides the uniqueness in the least rural cluster. A prime example of a unique aging experience in this zone cluster is in the area of caregiving.

Note the difference between zone clusters: 83 percent of baby boomers in the least rural zones talked about caregiving but only 32 percent of those in other zones did so. Not only is there a difference in how much caregiving, but also who the caregiving is for. Only one of the six baby boomers who shared stories of caregiving in the most rural and moderately rural RUCC zones spoke of children or grandchildren, the other five cared for elderly parents or loved ones. On the other hand, six of the ten in the less rural RUCC zone cluster spoke of caregiving for children or grandchildren, and four spoke of caring for elderly parents as their primary caregiving experience.

Aging in the less rural zone cluster has a key difference. There are more opportunities for caregiving, especially for grandchildren. While the baby boomers in the more rural zone clusters had largely experienced an outflow of their children and grandchildren for work and opportunities, the less rural baby boomers spoke of children and grandchildren who lived nearby. The result is the practical opportunity for the less rural residents to provide caregiving with aging, especially for younger generations.

Baby boomers referenced how their first interactions with the church that they affiliated with came through the third spaces and community rituals that they frequented. Don and Marge (3) spoke of how they became acquainted with their church through meeting church people at the village yard sale. Normative events such as community rituals provided them with first name contacts that grew into friendships.

Betty (3) was going through a series of non-normative crisis events in her life, and she found support through third spaces where period events consistently take place. Betty spoke of how local school events provided routine contact with people who befriended her and encouraged her. As she spent more time with this family, she eventually became comfortable affiliating with their church. The events were not overtly religious—they were public school sports and music events. But the size and proximity of the rural setting shaped the relationship component of these events so that religious belonging was eventually impacted.

# CHAPTER 16

# How I Generate Rural Ministry Barriers

N ow we summarize some of the fights that we should turn away from. Some of the most daunting barriers to effective rural ministry are facilitated by rural ministry practitioners themselves. Yes, you and I contribute to truncated rural ministry fruit because we are participants in three rural ministry past times: 1) the Arm Wrestling Effect, 2) the Green Acres Effect, and 3) the Pyramids Effect.

1. The Arm Wrestling Effect. Much has been written about the opportunities of ministry in metropolitan areas—and rightfully so. When it comes to discussion about rural ministry, the focus is generally on arm wrestling rather than advancing God's Kingdom. Arm wrestling is a winner-takes-all affair similar to rural ministry conferences. You know the arm wrestling deal: two seated competitors face one another with bent elbows and firmly clasp their hands together. Their gripped hands are fully upright at the start and then the goal is to pin the opponent's hand down to the table while keeping the hands clasped. There is a victor and a loser.

    When it comes to rural ministry, we often compare churches and pastors like an arm wrestling match. Who has the most people in a worship service, the most effective strategies for outreach, the largest virtual outreach—who is the alpha arm wrestler that outdoes all other competitors? What this inevitably leads to is the attempt to disqualify competitors because they are "not really rural." That ministry is actually in the suburbs, this ministry is too close to the urban fringe to count, this ministry is unique because it is an oasis in a rural desert of services.

We end up trying to discount kingdom advancing rural ministry as "not as rural as mine" because we do not take note of the diversity of rural experiences. We try to assess rural based on a monolithic measuring stick rather than a continuum. We need better rural context assessments.

In order to move beyond rural ministry arm wrestling and comparing ourselves against rural ministry contexts very different from our own, here are some simple steps that we can take to assess our own rural context:

a. Assess your county on a rural continuum. As previously highlighted, the United States Department of Agriculture provides an assessment of the level of rurality of your county. The "Rural-Urban Continuum Code" (RUCC) is a nine-point continuum where the higher the number, the higher level of rurality.[1] The continuum provides an idea of how disconnected a location is from urban influences. This is helpful to not only better understand your own context, but to also know rural ministries that are in similar contexts based on their RUCC. If you have not yet, please use this link: https://www.ers.usda.gov/data-products/rural-urban-continuum-codes.aspx

If your county is between a 2 and 3 on the continuum, it is likely to be rural refuge. The county is within a metropolitan area yet holds rural enclaves within it. You are likely to be in or near a small city, or in a bedroom community where most people travel to a nearby city for work and services. Yet, there are some third spaces to pay close attention to where "rural types" tend to congregate and interact. This might be a certain diner or a rural oriented supply store.

If your county is between a 4 and 6 on the continuum, it is likely to be rural sufficient. The county is outside metropolitan areas and is relatively self-supporting in regard to employment and services. Due to critical mass of population, there are plentiful services and community opportunities provided locally, leading churches to be more selective in their ministry outreach. Churches

1. USDA Economic Research Service, "Rural-Urban Continuum Codes." https://www.ers.usda.gov/data-products/rural-urban-continuum-codes/documentation.aspx

often opt to create their own third spaces in these settings to meet under reached populations and to provide a place where people can informally gather with consistency.

If your county is between a 7 and 9 on the continuum, you are likely to feel rural remote. Your county maintains low population density, low overall population, and is the greatest distance from urban centers. At the same time, because of the low population, there are minimal services provided by the public sector. Churches have great opportunity to meet unmet needs of local residents but may struggle with having the resources to match the need. While there is great missional opportunity in the community, it is likely that participating numbers will be low due to population of the area.

**Rural as a Continuum – Greene Adaptation**

| Zones 7 - 9 | Zones 4 - 6 | Zones 2 – 3 |
|---|---|---|
| **Remote** | **Rural Sufficient** | **Social Construction** |

| Open Space | Unincorporated Communities<br><br>Villages | Open Space<br><br>Uninc. Areas | Villages<br><br>Towns<br><br>Small Cities | Open Space<br><br>Uninc. Areas<br><br>Incorp. Municipalities |
|---|---|---|---|---|

Adapted with permission from "Rural as a Continuum" by Dr. Jeffrey Clark 2020.

b. Assess the space. County-based rural assessments can be deceiving. In order to have a better idea of the rurality of your specific space, it is important to look at *population density*. As rural ministry practitioners, we often assume that if we are not in a Census designated urban area (population of fifty thousand or more) then we must be in a monolithic rural experience, or we choose a lower population threshold of what is really rural! A better approach is more nuanced in assessing the specific space. The population of your space may be lower than an urbanized area (fifty thousand people), but even at a population of 2,500 it counts as an urban cluster in the eyes of the US Census Bureau.[2] To see if your ministry space has the population density to be considered an urban cluster, follow this link: https://www2.census.gov/geo/docs/reference/ua/ua_st_list_uc.xls.

The importance of knowing if you are in an urban cluster is not a matter of tarnishing the rural nature of your area. The purpose is to be able to honestly assess some of the unique features of your space. While there may be a rural subculture very much felt in your space, there are certain qualities that are different because of the critical mass of people living within proximity of one another. The prevalence of third spaces, community rituals, and social interactions will be much different in these spaces compared to less densely populated areas.

Another important item to assess is *land use*. This is tangentially linked with population density. If the church building or congregants live in a space where there is a preponderance of agricultural land, or state forests, or state parks, or natural amenities, there will be a certain flavor of rural to that area. There will be a certain assumed sub-culture of that space even if most people are not engaged in that economic activity. For instance, if a church is located in the middle of corn fields, there will be different rural assumptions than if it is located next to a heavily visited beach at a state park.

Clearly, assessing the space gets tricky. There is analyzation of where the church building is located, but some people might be from a densely populated village while others are from surrounding farms. This blend is another dynamic to be mindful of as you assess outgroups and the type of rural that people identify with—or the diversity of rural that your congregants might identify with.

c. Assess the place. Each place is unique. There is unique history, there are unique ethnic backdrops, and there are unique amenities. Some small places will host a university, some will host the headquarters of an international business, some will host the largest farm in the state, some will be economically declining, some

2. See   https://www.census.gov/programs-surveys/geography/guidance/geo-areas/urban-rural/2010-urban-rural.html for more details.

will be experiencing population growth. There is not a one-size-fits-all approach to rural assessments. There is a certain amount of *ground-truthing* that is essential to undertake. The key is to discover the unique attributes of your place and see how your church can creatively engage those attributes.

d. Stop competing. Rural ministry offers great missional opportunity. Rather than providing stories packed with numbers and metrics that do not translate across types of rural, we can do better at sharing stories about types of rural. When we begin to focus on type of rural, we begin to uncover the intersections of experience that we have with other rural places alongside the unique attributes of our specific rural ministry context. That is where much joy abounds.

2. The Green Acres Effect.[3] Green Acres was a television situational comedy in the 1960s that featured an upscale family from New York City moving to a rural farm in "Hooterville." The humor of the show in large part is driven by the obvious cultural divide between the non-native, formally dressed lawyer family from the city and the native, simpleton rural residents.

The Green Acres effect in our rural churches is the perpetuation of a cultural divide between "natives" and "non-natives." "New people" in the church can refer to lots of people: people who were not born in the town, retirees who recently moved to the area, families who have maintained a vacation home in town for thirty-five years and now live there full-time, an extended family of a different ethnicity than what is considered "normal."

While the television show highlights the conflict between natives and non-natives in Hooterville, it is much more nuanced in the rural church—but with similar effects. Without intentionality, clear outgroups are developed in the rural church. Leadership of the church, from the members of the diaconate and elders to the matriarch and patriarch powerbrokers of the church, are overwhelmingly natives. The non-natives are observed as important to be part of the community but are always on the outside looking in when it comes to the inner workings of the church.

3. Thank you to Dr. David M. Gustafson of Trinity International University for revealing the potential connection between modern rural outgroups and the fictional "Hooterville" of the 1960s.

The Green Acres effect is a two-way affair. The natives cast a jaded eye toward the newcomers as lacking "rural common sense." When a non-native slides off the road in the winter, gets their lawnmower stuck, or needs repairs for something they broke, it is because they are not really rural. At the same time, the non-natives can have an idyllic view of what rural life should be, but are consistently disappointed by their rural neighbors who, in their eyes, lack the sophistication and education to make well-reasoned decisions. The result is a "Hooterville" undertone of a divide between natives and non-natives.

When it comes to small groups within the church, the Green Acres effect is very pronounced. Small groups are an appealing option for non-natives looking for a place to belong. Since they do not have deep relational connections locally, the small groups offer many benefits not provided elsewhere, especially in a community that casts a jaded eye on newcomers. On the flip side though, natives are less likely to use small groups of the church because they already have their own extended family or friends as small groups.

The Green Acres effect can be best overcome when small groups are designed with intentionality to bring together natives and non-natives. The natives need to be aware that the small groups are not simply for their own benefit, and non-natives need to be equipped with rural sub-cultural sensitivity to be able to engage well on a relational level. A great way to bring people together is through service projects—opportunities where people can serve a greater purpose and begin to bridge the relational gap between natives and non-natives. This can also provide an effective pathway for leadership development and identification among people who did not "grow up in the church."

One of the most effective ways to erode the divide between natives and non-natives in large groups is through community rituals that are open for all to participate in—particularly funerals. Funerals are a place where community is expected to be supportive, and the division lines between native and non-native are less visible. Likewise, there are plenty of opportunities to be involved—especially preparing for and cleaning up after the meal.

3. The Pyramids Effect. The Pyramids of Egypt are old. Granted, they are really cool, but they are not exactly useful for practical purposes today. As we have already examined, the same is true for the population pyramid that rural churches continue to assume are a continuing reality.

There is no longer the traditional age pyramid; we are moving quickly to an age pillar—and that is especially true in rural America. The issue is our rural churches are staying focused on pyramid demographics.

## NEXT STEPS IN RURAL MINISTRY

We need to be self-aware of the three barriers that we participate in as rural ministry practitioners. First, rather than the *Arm Wrestling Effect*, we need to engage in rural context assessments that honor the diversity and specificity of rurality. Second, rather than living the *Green Acres Effect*, we need to be intentional about identifying and addressing out-groups that are within our communities and even our churches. Third, rather than assuming the *Pyramid Effect*, we need to go beyond an ageist approach to outreach where youth ministry is always assumed to be the answer. The early old age demographic is a tremendous silver mission opportunity that we are simply missing. There is great hope ahead in fruitful rural ministry, especially if we self-create fewer barriers.

# Epilogue

T HE shared tragedy of the Mann Gulch Wildfire reminds us of our need to maintain an ongoing posture of learning. The Smokejumper's reputation as fire experts prevented them from seeing what they did not know about a wildfire "blowup" that was taking place. As rural ministry practitioners, we are lured to consider rural ministry innovations prior to learning the people and place that we are immersed in. There is a fire to tend to in our community, and we want to jump into action. Although laudable, it can also be a recipe for a ministry disaster.

Part of my own story of rural ministry is the realization that I really do not know rural contexts as deeply as I assume I do. In fact, the older I get, the more I realize the complexities and specificities that contribute to the diversity of rural living, yet are beyond my personal experience. More than reading answers of "what rural is," I am now searching out tools to uncover what "rural are."[1] While acknowledging that there are rural generalities, we need the right tools to discover locality specific rural realities.

## DROPPING TOOLS

Hopefully, this book has revealed some ways that we can reconsider the identity of the rural church. Without intentionality, our desired identity of being an innovative rural church drives ministry more than what our rural demographics are telling us. Even more, we can focus only on stereotypes of our rural place rather than listening to the needs of the rural people themselves.

The Smokejumpers struggled to drop their tools. We are no different. The focused example of this book has been the understudied gospel

1. Thank you, Dr. Jeffrey Clark for this great adage.

opportunity presented by the Early Old Age (EOA) cultural phenomenon. If we hold on to the ministry tools of three decades ago, we will miss the present opportunity that is available to many rural communities. Hopefully the example of EOA provides similar thoughts for your context, but also opens the door of developing your own methodology to listen to your community for ministry opportunities beyond EOA.

## COMMUNICATION

The Smokejumpers saw their primary job as fire control and missed their responsibility to crew and safety. This led to broken communication patterns that contributed to a series of small, but cumulatively tragic decisions. In rural ministry, we are prone to do the same without upping our communication capacity.

Listening is one of the key areas that we need to work on. Rather than assuming that we know what we do not know, we need to develop listening patterns. One key method of listening is encouraging life review conversations with adults. Rather than assuming that people have no spiritual story until they have a polished testimony is a miss. It is when we listen to people's pre-evangelism stories that we get a sense of how God is at work in and through our community. We begin to sense how God is shaping individuals and drawing them to Himself across cumulative life experiences as individuals and as a community.

The listening needs to happen in safe places. We cannot wait until the noise of the fire and the rush of a crisis is so great that we can no longer hear well. We need to search out third spaces and create safe places for storytelling. Rather than assuming that our church offers a safe place for vulnerability and sharing, we need to dig deeper and uncover what might be holding us back.

And that brings us to communicating what we learn. We need to talk about the obvious. The Smokejumpers' crew foreman did not see the need to share the obvious with his crew. In his eyes, they should have been able to see that they were no longer in the forest, that the wind had changed, and that the fire was catching up with them. As rural ministry practitioners, we can often assume the same with our fellow church congregants.

We can assume that people know the demographics of our small town. We can assume that people grasp the cultural shift of Spiritual but Not Religious (SBNR). In fact, it is far too easy to become frustrated with our local church because she cannot see her need to adapt to the current context that she is in. I have unfortunately felt that frustration all too strongly—and only hurt my cause because I did not explain the "why." In fact, I did not even fully grasp the "why" myself.

Rather than jumping to the strategy of how the rural church needs to change, it is imperative that we explain just cause and build relational trust with our church family. When we begin to build the case of a cultural shift away from formal organizations toward more purpose driven, cause-oriented movements, we can lay the foundation for real problem solving. Rather than writing off the possibility of people "attending our church," we begin to reassess what belonging to church actually means and looks like. When we start grappling with faith commitment manifesting as the intersection of belonging, believing, and behaving, we move from pedantic strategy making to church identity reassessment.

## FIGHT THE RIGHT FIGHT

In rural ministry, I have found that we can fight like some of the wild animals here in my fair state of Wisconsin. We tend to go to the fierce extreme of the badger to the push over opossum. Like the badger, we can at times be ornery, solitary, and full of vinegar to have things our way. As the stereotype of a badger goes, everything rides on our ability to win the specific challenge on our terms. We are willing to fight for something insignificant and of no value in the grand scheme of things—but what we want.

At other times, when we face a difficulty we simply go opossum. We roll over and play dead. When we should stand up and fight for what is right, we play dead and hope that it goes away. The problem with the opossum approach is that our problem just festers and remains for when we open our eyes after a little nap.

As rural ministry practitioners, our work is not only in assessments and communication of truth. It is also prioritizing what matters most. We need to be able to sort through the data and highlight what matters most to our congregation. It is only then that we are able to fight the right fight, in the right ways.

After all, rural America is worth fighting for. Let's make the fight the right one. May God be honored and glorified as we join Him in this good work.

# Bibliography

Adams, Kevin J. *The Gospel in a Handshake: Framing Worship for Mission.* Eugene, OR: Cascade, 2019.

Alwin, Duane F. "Integrating Varieties of Life Course Concepts." *The Journals of Gerontology Series B: Psychological Sciences and Social Sciences.* 67.2 (2012) 206–20.

Ammerman, Nancy Tatom. *Congregation & Community.* New Brunswick, NJ: Rutgers University Press, 2001.

———. "Introduction: Observing Religious Modern Lives." In *Everyday Religion: Observing Modern Religious Lives,* edited by Nancy T. Ammerman, 3–18. Oxford: Oxford University Press, 2007.

———. "Rethinking Religion: Toward a Practice Approach." *American Journal of Sociology.* 126.1 (2020) 6–51.

———. "Spiritual But Not Religious? Beyond Binary Choices in the Study of Religion." *Journal for the Scientific Study of Religion* 52.2 (2013) 258–78.

Baltes, Matilda M., and Laura L. Carstensen. "The Process of Successful Ageing." *Ageing and Society* 16 (1996) 397–422.

Baltes, Paul B. "Theoretical Propositions of Life-Span Developmental Psychology: On the Dynamics Between Growth and Decline." *Developmental Psychology* 23.5 (1987) 611–26.

Baltes, Paul B., et al. "Life Span Theory in Developmental Psychology." In *The Handbook of Child Psychology: Theoretical Models of Human Development,* edited by Richard M. Lerner, 1:569–659. 6th ed. New York: Wiley, 2006.

Bell, Michael M. "The Fruit of Difference: The Rural-Urban Continuum as a System of Identity." *Rural Sociology* 57.1 (1992) 65–82.

Bellah, Robert. "Civil Religion in America." *Daedalus* 96.1 (1967) 1–21. http://www.jstor.org/stable/20027022.

Bengtson, Vern L., et al. "Older Adults in Churches: Differences in Perceptions of Clergy and Older Members." *Journal of Religion, Spirituality, and Aging* 30.2 (2018) 154–78.

Bengtson, Vern L., et al. "Does Religiousness Increase with Age? Age Changes and Generational Differences Over 35 Years." *Journal for the Scientific Study of Religion* 54.2 (2015) 363–79.

Beyerlein, Kraig, and John R. Hipp. "Social Capital, Too Much of a Good Thing? American Religious Traditions and Community Crime." *Social Forces* 84 (2005) 995–1013.

Breen, Mike. *Leading Missional Communities: Rediscovering the Power of Living on Mission Together.* Pawleys Island, SC: 3DM, 2013.

Brewer, Marilynn B., and Wendi Gardner. "Who Is This 'We'? Levels of Collective Identity and Self Representations." *Journal of Personality and Social Psychology* 71.1 (1996) 83–93.

Brown, David L., and Kai A. Schafft.. *Rural People and Communities in the 21st Century: Resilience and Transformation.* Cambridge, UK: Polity, 1996.

Butler, Robert N. "The Life Review: An Interpretation of Reminiscence in the Aged." *Psychiatry* 26.1 (1963) 65–76. DOI: 10.1080/00332747.1963.11023339.

Carey, James R. "Life Span: A Conceptual Overview." *Population and Development Review.* 29 (2003) 1–18.

Carstensen, Laura L. *A Long Bright Future: Happiness, Health, and Financial Security in an Age of Increased Longevity.* New York: Broadway, 2011.

Castree, Noel, and Bruce Braun. "Constructing Rural Natures." In *Handbook of Rural Studies,* edited by Paul Cloke et al., 161–70. London: SAGE, 2006.

Cilliers, Johan, and Cas Wepener. "Ritual and the Generation of Social Capital in Contexts of Poverty: A South African Exploration." *International Journal of Practical Theology* 11.1 (2007) 39–55.

Cloke, Paul. "Conceptualizing Rurality." In *Handbook of Rural Studies,* edited by Paul Cloke et al., 18–28. London: SAGE, 2006.

Cnaan, Ram A., et al. "Religious Congregations as Social Services Providers for Older Adults." *Journal of Gerontological Social Work* 45.1-2 (2005) 105–30.

Coleman, James S. "Social Capital in the Creation of Human Capital." *American Journal of Sociology* 94 (1988) S95–S120.

Cromartie, John. *Historical Development of ERS Rural Urban Classifications Systems.* Paper presented at the Workshop on Rationalizing Rural Area Classifications, April, National Academies of Sciences, Engineering, and Medicine, Washington, DC. In National Academies of Sciences, Engineering, and Medicine. 2016. *Rationalizing Rural Area Classifications for the Economic Research Service: Workshop Summary.* G.S. Wunderlich, *Rapporteur,* Committee on National Statistics. Division of Behavioral and Social Sciences and Education. Washington, DC: The National Academies Press.

Curry, Janel. "Social Capital and Societal Vision: A Study of Six Farm Communities in Iowa." In *Religion as Social Capital: Producing the Common Good,* ed. Corwin Smidt, 139–52. Waco, TX: Baylor University Press, 2003.

Davie, Grace. *Religion in Britain: A Persistent Paradox,* 2nd ed. West Sussex, UK: Wiley Blackwell, 2015.

———. *Religion in Britain Since 1945: Believing Without Belonging.* Oxford–Cambridge, MA: Blackwell, 1994.

Dillon, Michele, and Paul Wink. *In the Course of a Lifetime: Tracing Religious Belief, Practice, and Change.* Berkeley: University of California Press, 2007.

Durkheim, Emile. *The Rules of Sociological Method.* Translated by W. D. Halls. New York: Free Press, 1982.

Edward, Joyce. "Friends in Old Age." *Clinical Social Work Journal* 44 (2016) 198–203.

English, Tammy, and Laura L. Carstensen. "Selective Narrowing of Social Networks Across Adulthood Is Associated with Improved Emotional Experience in Daily Life." *International Journal of Behavioral Development* 38.2 (2014) 195–202.

Erikson, Eric H., and Joan M. Erikson. *The Life Cycle Completed: Extended Version with New Chapters on the Ninth Stage of Development.* New York: Norton, 1998.

Fine, Gary Allen, and Sherryl Kleinman. "Rethinking Subculture: An Interactionist Analysis." *American Journal of Sociology* 85.1 (1979) 1–20.

# Bibliography

Finney, John. *Recovering the Past: Celtic and Roman Mission*. London: Darton, Longman, and Todd, 1996.

Fischer, Claude S. "The Subcultural Theory of Urbanism: A Twentieth-Year Assessment." *American Journal of Sociology* 101.3 (1995) 543–77.

Fosse, Ethan, and Christopher Winship. "Analyzing Age-Period-Cohort Data: A Review and Critique." *Annual Review of Sociology* 45 (2019) 467–92.

Fu, Wenjiang. *A Practical Guide to Age-Period-Cohort Analysis: The Identification Problem and Beyond*. CRC, Ebook Central, 2018. https://ebookcentral.proquest.com/lib/tiu/detail.action?docID=5372016.

Fung, Helene H. "Aging in Culture." *The Gerontologist* 53.3 (2013 369–77.

Gelder, Ken. "The Field of Subcultural Studies." In *The Subcultures Reader*, edited by Ken Gelder, 1–18. New York: Routledge, 2005.

Granovetter, Mark S. "The Strength of Weak Ties." *American Journal of Sociology* 78 (1973) 1360–80.

Greene, Carl. "U.S. Baby Boomers Experiencing Increased Christian Religiosity: The Influence of Age, Period, Cohort, and Rural Context." PhD diss., 2021. Trinity Evangelical Divinity School.

Greene, Carl. *A Hunger to Belong: Welcoming Baby Boomers Back to the Table*. Janesville, WI: Seventh Day Baptist General Conference, 2020.

Gregory, Meredith, and Caitlin Finlayson. "The Paradox of Cracker Barrel: A Case Study on Place and Placelessness." *Advances in Hospitality and Tourism Research* 7.2 (2019) 258–76.

Gustafson, David M. *Gospel Witness: Evangelism in Word & Deed*. Grand Rapids: Eerdmans, 2019.

Halfacree, Keith. "Locality and Social Representation: Space, Discourse and Alternative Definitions of the Rural." *Journal of Rural Studies* 9.1 (1993) 23–37.

———. "Rethinking Rurality." In *New Forms of Urbanization: Beyond the Urban-Rural Dichotomy*, edited by Tony Champion and Graeme Hugo, 285–304. Aldershot, Hants, England: Ashgate, 2004.

———. "Rural Space: Constructing a Three-fold Architecture." In *Handbook of Rural Studies*, edited by Paul Cloke et al., 18–28. London: SAGE, 2006.

———. E-mail message to author. January 13, 2020.

Hall, Edward T. *The Hidden Dimension*. Garden City, NY: Anchor Books/Doubleday, 1982.

———. "Proxemics." *Current Anthropology* 9.2/3 (1968) 83–108.

Harrington, Bobby, and Alex Absalom. *Discipleship that Fits: The Five Kinds of Relationships God Uses to Help Us Grow*. Grand Rapids: Zondervan, 2016.

Harris, Frederick. "Ties That Bind and Flourish: Religion as Social Capital in African-American Politics." In *Religion as Social Capital: Producing the Common Good*, edited by Corwin Smidt, 121–38. Waco, TX: Baylor University Press, 2003.

Hayward, R. David, and Neal Krause. "Aging, Social Developmental, and Cultural Factors in Changing Patterns of Religious Involvement Over a 32-Year Period: An Age-Period-Cohort Analysis of 80 Countries." *Journal of Cross-Cultural Psychology* 46.8 (2015) 979–95.

———. "Changes in Church-Based Social Support Relationships During Older Adulthood." *Journals of Gerontology Series B: Psychological Sciences and Social Sciences* 68.1 (2013) 85–96.

———. "Patterns of Change in Religious Service Attendance Across the Life Course: Evidence From a 34-Year Longitudinal Study." *Social Science Research* 42 (2013) 1480–89.

———. "Religion, Health, and Aging." In *Handbook of Aging and the Social Sciences*, edited by Linda K. George et al., 251–70. Handbooks of Aging Series. 8th ed. Boston: Academic, 2016 .

Henderson, Lauren, et al. "The Silver Tsunami: Evaluating the Impact of Population Aging in the U.S." *Journal of Business and Behavioral Sciences* 29.2 (2017) 155–69.

Herd, Pamela, et al. "Cohort Profile: Wisconsin Longitudinal Study (WLS)." *International Journal of Epidemiology* 43 (2014) 34–41.

Herzog, Patricia Snell. "Youth and Emerging Adults: The Changing Contexts of Faith and Giving." *Religions* 8.124 (2017) 1–10. DOI: 10.3390/rel8070124 www.mdpi.com/journal/religions.

Herzog, Patricia Snell, and De Andre Beadle. "Emerging Adult Religiosity and Spirituality: Linking Beliefs, Values, and Ethical Decision-Making." *Religions* 9.84 (2018) 1–18.

Hoggart, Keith, and Henry Buller. *Rural Development: A Geographical Perspective.* London: Croom Helm, 1987.

Hollinghurst, Steve. *Mission-Shaped Evangelism: The Gospel in Contemporary Culture.* Norwich, UK: Canterbury, 2010.

Howse. K. *Religion, Spirituality, and Older People.* London: Centre for Policy on Ageing, 1999.

Hunter, James Davidson. "What Is Modernity? Historical Roots and Contemporary Features." In *Faith and Modernity,* edited by P. Sampson et al., 12–28. Oxford: Regnum Books International, 1994.

Ingraham, Christopher. *If You Lived Here You'd Be Home by Now: Why We Traded the Commuting Life for a Little House on the Prairie.* New York: Harper Paperbacks, 2020.

Kaemingk, Matthew, and Cory B. Wilson. *Work and Worship.* Ada, MI: Baker Academic, 2020.

Keller, Tim. *Every Good Endeavor: Connecting Your Work to God's Work.* London: Penguin, 2012.

Kersten, Nicholas J. Interview by author. Janesville, WI. November 13, 2019. In *A Hunger to Belong: Welcoming Baby Boomers Back to the Table* by Carl Greene. Janesville, WI: Seventh Day Baptist General Conference.

Lehman, Eben. "August 5, 1949: Mann Gulch Tragedy. Forest History Society." (August 5, 2009) https://foresthistory.org/august-5-1949-mann-gulch-tragedy/.

Lichter, Daniel, and David Brown. "Rural America in an Urban Society: Changing Spatial and Social Boundaries." *Annual Review of Sociology* 37 (2011) 565–92.

Lichter, Daniel, and James Ziliak. "The Rural-Urban Interface: New Patterns of Spatial Interdependence and Inequality in America." *Annals, American Association of Political and Social Science* 672 (2017) 6–25.

Lichter, Daniel, et al. "The Rural-Urban Interface: Rural and Small Town Growth at the Metropolitan Fringe." *Population, Space, and Place* (2020) 1–14.

Lipka, Michael, and Claire Gecewicz. "More Americans Now Say They're Spiritual But Not Religious." April 6, 2017. https://www.pewresearch.org/fact-tank/2017/09/06/more-americans-now-say-theyre-spiritual-but-not-religious/.

Maclean, Norman. *Young Men and Fire.* Chicago: University of Chicago Press, 1992.

Maselko, Joanna, et al. "Religious Social Capital: Its Measurement and Utility in the Study of Social Determinants of Health." *Social Science and Medicine* 73 (2011) 759–67.

# BIBLIOGRAPHY

McIntosh, Gary. "Trends and Challenges for Ministry Among North America's Largest Generation." *Christian Education Journal, Series 3* 5.2 (2008) 294–304.

McNeal, Reggie. "Missional Communities—European Style." In *Missional Communities: The Rise of the Post-Congregational Church*, 39–64. San Francisco: Jossey-Bass, 2011.

Mills, Marie A., et al. "Listening and Enabling the Sharing of Beliefs and Values in Later Life." In *Belief and Ageing: Spiritual Pathways in Later Life*, edited by Peter G. Coleman, 35-58. Bristol, UK: Policy, 2011.

Moon, Jay, and W. Bud Simon. *Effective Intercultural Evangelism: Good News in a Diverse World*. Downers Grove, IL: InterVarsity, 2021.

Murphy, James. "Beyond 'Religion' and 'Spirituality': Extending a 'Meaning Systems' Approach to Explore Lived Religion." *Archive for the Psychology of Religion* (2017). DOI 10.1163/15736121-12341335. 1-26.

Myers, Joseph R. *Organic Community: Creating a Place Where People Naturally Connect*. Grand Rapids: Baker, 2007.

———. *The Search to Belong: Rethinking Intimacy, Community, and Small Groups*. Grand Rapids: Zondervan, 2003.

Newbigin, Lesslie. *The Gospel in a Pluralist Society*. London: SPCK, 1989.

Novack, Janet. "8 Ways Coronavirus Will Drastically Alter Boomer Retirements." *Forbes*, March 16, 2020. https://www.forbes.com/sites/janetnovack/2020/03/16/8-ways-coronavirus-will-drastically-alter-boomer-retirements/#405aabe53474.

Olson, Laura R., and Adam L. Warber. "Belonging, Behaving, and Believing: Assessing the Role of Religion on Presidential Approval." *Political Research Quarterly* 61.2 (2008) 192–204.

Panelli, Ruth. "Rural Society." In *Handbook of Rural Studies*, edited by Paul Cloke et al., 63–90. London: SAGE, 2006.

Patrick, Carlianne. Statement at ERS Workshop (2015). In National Academies of Sciences, Engineering, and Medicine. 2016. *Rationalizing Rural Area Classifications for the Economic Research Service: Workshop Summary*. G.S. Wunderlich, *Rapporteur*, Committee on National Statistics. Division of Behavioral and Social Sciences and Education. Washington, DC: The National Academies Press.

Paxton, Pamela. "Is Social Capital Declining in the United States? A Multiple Indicator Assessment." *American Journal of Sociology* 105.1 (1999) 88–127.

Peabody, Larry. *God Loves Your Work: Discover Why He Send You to Do What You Do*. Eugene, OR: Wipf & Stock, 2022.

Peddle, Geoff. "Rural Anglicanism in Newfoundland: Signs of Social Capital and Intrinsic Religiosity." *Rural Theology* 11.1 (2013) 15-27.

Peterson, Andrew. *The God of the Garden*. Nashville: B&H, 2021.

Portes, Alejandro. "Social Capital: Its Origins and Applications in Modern Sociology." *Annual Review of Sociology* 24 (1998) 1–24.

Putnam, Robert D. *Bowling Alone: The Collapse and Revival of American Community*. New York: Simon & Schuster, 2000.

Putnam, Robert D., and David E. Campbell. *American Grace: How Religion Divides and Unites Us*. New York: Simon & Schuster, 2010.

Ramsey, Janet L., and Rosemary Blieszner. *Spiritual Resiliency and Aging: Hope, Relationality, and the Creative Self*. Amityville, NY: Baywood, 2013.

Relph, E. C. *Place and Placelessness*. London: Pion, 1976.

Richardson, Richard. *You Found Me: New Research on How Unchurched Nones, Millennials, and Irreligious Are Surprisingly Open to Christian Faith.* Downers Grove, IL: InterVarsity, 2019.

Riley, Matilda White. "Aging and Cohort Succession: Interpretations and Misinterpretations." *The Public Opinion Quarterly* 37 (1973) 35–49.

———. "On the Significance of Age in Sociology." American Sociological Review 52.1 (1987) 1–14.

Roesch-McNally, Gabrielle, et al. "Soil as Social-Ecological Feedback: Examining the 'Ethic' of Soil Stewardship among Corn Belt Farmers." *Rural Sociology* 83.1 (2018) 145–73.

Rolph, Paul, et al. "What Churches May Have to Learn from an Aging Population." *Rural Theology* 15.2 (2017) 60–73.

Rose, Arnold M. "The Subculture of the Aging: A Topic for Sociological Research." *The Gerontologist* 2.3 (1962) 123–27.

Rudolph, Cort W., and Hannes Zacher. "'The COVID-19 Generation': A Cautionary Note." *Work, Aging and Retirement* 6.3 (2020) 139–45. https://doi.org/10.1093/workar/waaa009.

Schulz, Kathryn. "The Story That Tore Through the Trees." *New York Magazine.* September 9, 2014. https://nymag.com/arts/books/features/mann-gulch-norman-maclean-2014-9/index.html.

Schwadel, Philip. "Age, Period, and Cohort Effects on Religious Activities and Beliefs." *Social Science Research* 40 (2011) 181–92.

Seversen, Beth. "Millennials Connecting to Contemporary Congregations: Effectively Reaching and Incorporating Emerging Adults in North American Evangelical Covenant Churches. PhD diss., 2017, Trinity Evangelical Divinity School.

Shucksmith, Mark. Statement at ERS Workshop (2015). In National Academies of Sciences, Engineering, and Medicine. 2016. *Rationalizing Rural Area Classifications for the Economic Research Service: Workshop Summary.* G.S. Wunderlich, *Rapporteur,* Committee on National Statistics. Division of Behavioral and Social Sciences and Education. Washington, DC: The National Academies Press.

Shucksmith, Mark, and David L. Brown. "Framing Rural Studies in the Global North." In *Routledge International Handbook of Rural Studies,* edited by Mark Shucksmith and David L. Brown, 1–16. New York: Routledge, 2016.

Silverstein, Merril, and Vern L. Bengtson. "Return to Religion? Predictors of Religious Change Among Baby-Boomers in the Transition to Later Life." *Journal of Population Ageing* 11 (2018) 7–21.

Smith, Christian, with Patricia Snell. *Souls in Transition: The Religious and Spiritual Lives of Emerging Adults.* New York: Oxford University Press, 2009.

Smith, James K. A. *Who's Afraid of Postmodernism? Taking Derrida, Lyotard and Foucault to Church.* Grand Rapids, MI: Baker Academic, 2006.

Stark, Rodney, and Roger Finke. *Acts of Faith: Explaining the Human Side of Religion.* Berkley: University of California Press, 2000.

Strauss, William, and Neil Howe. *Generations: The History of America's Future, 1584-2069.* New York: William Morrow, 1992.

Streib, Heinz, and Ralph W. Hood. "'Spirituality' as Privatized Experience-Oriented Religion: Empirical and Conceptual Perspectives." *Implicit Religion* 14.4 (2011) 433–53.

Streib, Heinz, et al. "Deconversion and 'Spirituality"—Migrations in the Religious Field." In *Semantics and Psychology of Spirituality: A Cross-Cultural Analysis*, edited by Heinz Streib and Ralph W. Hood, 19–26. Switzerland: Springer, 2016.

Swart, Ignatius. "Social Capital, Religious Social Capital and the Missing Element of Religious Ritual." *Religion & Theology: A Journal of Contemporary Discourse* 24 (2017) 221–49.

Swenson, Donald. *Society, Spirituality, and the Sacred: A Social Scientific Introduction.* Toronto, Canada: Toronto University Press, 2009.

Taylor, Daniel. *Tell Me a Story: The Life-Shaping Power of Our Stories.* St. Paul, MN: Bog Walk, 2001.

Tergesen, Anne. "How Covid-19 Will Change Aging and Retirement: Among Other Things, Expect More Aging in Place and a Wave of Innovation to Help Make That Happen." *Wall Street Journal*, November 15, 2020. https://www.wsj.com/articles/how-covid-19-will-change-aging-and-retirement-11605452401.

Thomas, Troy D., et al. "Response Styles and the Rural-Urban Divide." *Educational and Psychological Measurement* 74.1 (2014) 97–115.

Tornstam, Lars. "Maturing Into Gerotranscendence." *The Journal of Transpersonal Psychology* 43.2 (2011) 166–80.

Tuan, Yi-Fu. *Space and Place: The Perspective of Experience.* Minneapolis: University of Minnesota Press, 1977.

Turner, Dave. "The Thirteenth Fire." *Forest History Today*, 1999. https://foresthistory.org/wp-content/uploads/2017/02/The-Thirteenth-Fire.pdf.

United States Census Bureau. "2030 Marks Important Demographic Milestones for U.S. Population." Revision of Press Release CB18-41. September 6, 2018. https://www.census.gov/newsroom/press-releases/2018/cb18-41-population-projections.html.

———. "An Aging Nation: Projected Number of Children and Older Adults." March 13, 2018. https://www.census.gov/library/visualizations/2018/comm/historic-first.html.

———. "From Pyramid to Pillar: A Century of Change." March 13, 2018. https://www.census.gov/library/visualizations/2018/comm/century-of-change.html.

United States Department of Agriculture Economic Research Service. 2018. "Rural America at a Glance, 2018 Edition." Economic Information Bulletin 200. November 2018. https://www.ers.usda.gov/webdocs/publications/90556/eib-200.pdf?v=5899.2.

———. "Rural-Urban Continuum Codes." https://www.ers.usda.gov/data-products/rural- urban-continuum-codes/documentation.aspx.

United States Department of the Interior, USGS. "How Many Counties are in the United States?" https://www.usgs.gov/faqs/how-many-counties-are-united-states?qt-news_science_products=0#qt-news_science_products.

Vanderstelt, Jeff. *Saturate: Being Disciples of Jesus in the Everyday Stuff of Life.* Wheaton, IL: Crossway, 2015.

Webber, Robert E. *Ancient-Future Evangelism: Making Your Church a Faith-Forming Community.* Grand Rapids: Baker, 2003.

Weick, Karl E. "Drop Your Tools: An Allegory for Organizational Studies." *Administrative Science Quarterly* 41.2 (1996) 301–13.

Weil, Joyce. *Research Design in Again and Social Gerontology: Quantitative, Qualitative, and Mixed Methods.* New York: Routledge, 2017.

Whalen, Andrew. "What Is 'Boomer Remover" and Why is it Making People So Angry? *Newsweek*, March 13, 2020. https://www.newsweek.com/boomer-remover-meme-trends-virus-coronavirus-social-media-covid-19-baby-boomers-1492190.

# Bibliography

Williams, J. Patrick. *Subculture Theory: Traditions and Concepts.* Malden, MA: Polity, 2011.

Wirth, Louis. "Urbanism as a Way of Life." *American Journal of Sociology* 44.1 (1938) 1–24.

Wisconsin Longitudinal Study (WLS). "Graduates, Siblings, and Spouses: 1957-2020." Version 13.08. Machine-readable data file. Hauser, Robert M., William H. Sewell, and Pamela Herd as Principal Investigator(s). Madison, WI: University of Wisconsin-Madison, WLS. http://www.ssc.wisc.edu/wlsresearch/documentation/.

Woods, Michael. *Conceptualizing Rural Areas in Metropolitan Society: A Rural View.* Paper presented at the Workshop on Rationalizing Rural Area Classifications, April 2015, National Academies of Sciences, Engineering, and Medicine, Washington, DC. http://sites.nationalacademies.org/DBASSE/CNSTAT/DBASSE_160632 .

———. *Rural.* Key Ideas in Geography Series. Edited by Sarah Holloway and Gill Valentine. New York: Routledge, 2011.

Woolcock, Michael. "The Place of Social Capital in Understanding Social and Economic Outcomes." *ISUMA:Canadian Journal of Policy Research* 2 (2001) 1–35.

Wuthnow, Robert. *What Happens When We Practice Religion? Textures of Devotion in Everyday Life.* Princeton: Princeton University Press, 2020.

www.ingramcontent.com/pod-product-compliance
Lightning Source LLC
Chambersburg PA
CBHW061736270326
41928CB00011B/2261